Tastes and Tales
of a Chef

Stories and Recipes

*Enjoy my Tales and Tastes
have fun*

Frederic H. Sonnenschmidt

*CMC
2010*

PEARSON

Prentice
Hall

Upper Saddle River, New Jersey, 07458

Library of Congress Cataloging-in-Publication Data

Sonnenschmidt, Frederic H.
   Tastes and tales of a chef : stories and recipes / Frederic H.
Sonnenschimdt.
      p. cm.
   ISBN 0-13-112225-8
   1. Cookery. 2. Cookery—Anecdotes. 3. Sonnenschmidt, Frederic H.,
1935—Anecdotes. I. Title.
   TX714.S617 2003
   641.5—dc21

2003012096

Editor-in-Chief: Stephen Helba
Executive Editor: Vernon R. Anthony
Executive Assistant: Nancy Kesterson
Editorial Assistant: Ann Brunner
Director of Manufacturing and Production:
   Bruce Johnson
Managing Editor: Mary Carnis
Production Liaison: Adele M. Kupchik
Manufacturing Manager: Ilene Sanford
Manufacturing Buyer: Cathleen Petersen
Interior Design & Formatting: Pine Tree
   Composition, Inc.

Production Editor: John Shannon/Pine Tree
   Composition, Inc.
Cover Designer: Christopher Weigand
Cover Image: Lorna Smith
Marketing Manager: Ryan DeGrote
Marketing Assistant: Elizabeth Farrell
Senior Marketing Coordinator: Adam Kloza
Printer/Binder: Phoenix Book Tech
Cover Printer: Phoenix Book Tech

Pearson Education LTD.
Pearson Education Australia PTY, Limited
Pearson Education Singapore, Pte. Ltd
Pearson Education North Asia Ltd

Pearson Education, Canada, Ltd.
Pearson Educación de Mexico, S.A. de C.V.
Pearson Education—Japan
Pearson Education Malaysia, Pte. Ltd

10 9 8 7 6 5 4 3 2 1
ISBN 0-13-112225-8

Contents

Supervisory Development

The Curse of the Pastry Chef

The Incident

One Roast Beef ... and Hold the Piccadilly, or How Sherlock Holmes and a Roast Beef Sandwich Were Responsible for Me Becoming an American

The Ghost

Foreword

I met Fritz Sonnenschmidt the first day I set foot on the campus of the Culinary Institute of America (CIA), his employer for 34 years until his retirement in 2002. I ate my lamb shank at the American Bounty restaurant and he regaled me with stories—the man is filled with stories of life in the professional kitchen. He was also filled, I would find, with an extraordinary depth of cooking knowledge.

I would also discover that the student body and staff respected him greatly as one of the godfathers of the school and as a knowledgeable culinarian. I wrote about a cooking test at the CIA taken by outsiders, and I learned what working chefs thought of the man when I asked the chef preparing for the charcuterie section of the test if he were just making a terrine.

"When you're making a terrine for Chef Sonnenschmidt, who is a world authority on terrines," the candidate told me, "it's not *just* a terrine." Indeed, Sonnenschmidt is an expert and authority on the culinary specialties charcuterie and garde manger—pâtés, sausages, sauces, salads, canapés—and an author of a book on the subject.

Chef Sonnenschmidt was born in 1935 in Munich, Germany, and began his culinary career in 1952 as a cook at Restaurant Rolandseck in Munich; then, in 1955, he moved to Bayerischer Hof as chef de cuisine. He soon moved to London were he cooked at the Picadilly Hotel and the Grosvenor Hotel, before traveling to the United States, where he has lived since.

This of course is a bare description of a long and rich culinary career out of which the stories and recipes in this volume arise and omits the meaningful details that truly describe Sonnenschmidt, who is large in girth and larger in spirit. These stories come from a chef who began cooking in and on coal-fed ranges and follow his quirky, diverse path through the world of professional cooking and the work of cooking instruction; the recipes range from basic crepes to Moroccan couscous, to classical French preparations, to a recipe for camel steaks to the best paste for cleaning copper pots. And many of the stories conclude with lessons, reflecting the work that has occupied most of Chef Sonnenschmidt's career, that of a teacher.

In person, Sonnenschmidt is a delight, and his voice resonates clearly in these tales. But more important than the recipes, of course, more important than the individual tales, is what underlies this work: the man's every syllable emanates from a spirit founded on the work of giving, the giving of story, the giving of information, the giving of food, nourishing mind and spirit. Cooking is all about giving, all about making people happy. Chef Sonnenschmidt, a cook, a chef, a raconteur, embodies the fundamental spirit of generosity that is at the heart of great cooking.

Michael Ruhlman, June 2003
Author of *The Making of a Chef:*
Mastering Heat at the Culinary Institute of America
and *The Soul of the Chef: The Journey Toward Perfection*

Preface

Cooking is an Art and a Way of Life

I dedicate this book to all the chefs, professional and amateur, and to everyone who believes in life. Like art, food is a stimulus to people, but more importantly, it is the essence of life.

I hope you see yourself in my "tales" and have fun cooking with the help of the recipes wherever you are. Sit down with family and friends and share your passion for cooking with them. I believe if more people would take just 1 hour and 20 minutes out of their daily lives and cook a simple and easy meal, most of our problems would disappear. So enjoy the aromas, the colors and the textures of your food, and spin your tales. The reward will be a taste so great that it will give you peace of mind, health, and enjoyment.

Frederic H. (for humble) Sonnenschmidt

Acknowledgments

I like to thank all the chefs who gave me the basics to become successful; my wife Debbie for tasting all the recipes and gaining weight; my in-laws, father and Mother Prislopski, for allowing me to marry their daughter; Lorna Smith for taking my picture and making me look thin; and Maryann Monachelli, the only person who can read my handwriting, for typing the book. I also want to thank Prentice Hall for publishing it, and a special thank-you to you, the reader of my stories.

Fritz (not on the fritz, but always on the mend) Sonnenschmidt

Tastes and Tales of a Chef

Stories and Recipies

Tales of a Chef

In my previous life, if there was one, I must have lived and cooked in Egypt, a country of ancient civilization, history, and lots of mysteries. The Egyptian chef Epainetos, creator of the first forcemeat in 75 B.C., inspired me, as well Mr. Sherlock Holmes. In the manner of Mr. Holmes, I followed Epainetos's culinary footsteps and ended up in Egypt. I felt at home in Egypt. The food, the people, and, of course, the pyramids gave the country a feeling of greatness.

We tasted all the native foods and drinks. I remember one drink in particular. It was an old Egyptian love potion that was to be taken during a full moon in the shadow of the pyramids. The recipe was a secret, but I uncovered the papyrus on which it was written: 1 pint of water from the Nile, 1 ounce of mashed licorice root, 1 ounce of pureed sesame seeds, 1 ounce of bruised fennel seeds, and some honey. It worked, but not as I thought it would work! The potion invoked the curse of King Montezuma . . . and here starts my tale. . . .

After drinking the potion in the shadow of the pyramid at a full moon, we decided to research the ancient legends concerning the power food had over the Pharaohs. To do this, we planned to visit the tombs and look for evidence of onion, garlic, laurel leaf, and all the other food secrets hidden in the tombs. We hired a guide and some camels to ride in style. I bought myself a real native outfit: a fez, a djellaba, dark sunglasses, and a weddel to keep the flies away, and, of course, some sandals. I looked good as we took off. Now, if you never rode a camel, it's definitely a live experience. First, you mount the animal. Then you hold on for your life. I did not—I fell off. My sunglasses bent, and my fez bent out of shape. I mounted the camel again. It went up from behind, then from the front; it was a backlash, and my bones cracked. It was then I felt King Montezuma call.

The camel started to walk and sounds came from the front: "ayah, ayah." The smell of 1,000 years of teeth that haven't been brushed followed with a rumbling feeling from within the brute, like a small earthquake. (I guess a camel's digestive system works differently.) This was followed by an explosive sound from the back, like a Mercedes racing the Indy 500, and an aroma beyond explanation. I sat in the crosswind of both front and back when Monte hit me. I yelled, "Stop!"

The camel came to a shrieking halt in the sand and went down onto its front legs like Father Murphy's elevator in Roth Hall. I stood there in the desert being hit by my friend Montezuma front and back, if you get my meaning! I arrived at the base of the pyramid smelling like the camel. (I have used extra-strong Brut cologne ever since.)

The moral of the tale is always watch what you drink and eat!

Choukchouka Vegetable Appetizer
(10 portions)

Ingredients

8 oz.	Onions, sliced
5 oz.	Olive oil
3 lb.	Small eggplants, sliced 1-inch thick
3½ lb.	Zucchini, sliced 1-inch thick
2 lb.	Green peppers, seeded and sliced
2 lb.	Tomatoes, cores removed and sliced into 1-inch pieces
3	Garlic cloves, chopped
Some	Salt and pepper
10	Eggs

Method

Preheat oven to 350–400 degrees F.

Heat 2 oz. of olive oil in a casserole. Add sliced onions and sauté for 2 minutes.

Add eggplant, zucchini, green peppers, and tomatoes in layers.

Add garlic, salt, pepper, and the rest of the olive oil.

Cover and braise in preheated oven for 1 hour.

Crack eggs into the pan, placing them side by side.

Season with salt and pepper and return the pan to the oven. Cook until the eggs are done.

Serve warm.

Camel Steaks with Eggplants
(10 portions)

Ingredients

4 lb.	Camel loin (just kidding—you can use filet of beef)
To taste	Salt and pepper
1 oz.	Lemon juice
5 oz.	Olive oil
4 oz.	Shallots, finely chopped
3	Garlic cloves, finely chopped
6 oz.	White wine or beef broth
12 oz.	Tomato concasse
4 large	Eggplants
1 tbsp.	Flour
3 oz.	Butter

Method

Trim loin and cut into 20 medallions or steaks.

Season with salt and pepper.

Combine 2 oz. of oil and lemon juice and marinate steaks for 1 to 2 hours.

Heat the rest of the oil and sauté steaks to desired doneness. Remove steaks from pan and place on a warm plate.

Add shallots and garlic to pan and sauté for 1 minute.

Add white wine or beef broth and reduce by two-thirds.

Add tomato concasse.

Season with salt and pepper and sauté for 3 minutes. Set aside.

Cut eggplants into 20 even tranches

Season with salt and pepper.

Dust with flour and sauté in butter until golden on each side.

Place steak on eggplant and cover with tomato concasse.

Serve with rice or couscous.

Koschaf (Mixed Fruits) with Dotted Cream

Ingredients

1 lb.	Dried apricots
1 lb.	Dried figs
1 lb.	Dried dates
5 oz.	Raisins
5 oz.	Currants
7 oz.	Almonds
3 oz.	Pistachios
7 oz.	Sugar
2 tbsp.	Orange flower water or juice

Method

Wash all the dried fruits.

Cover with water and add sugar.

Bring to a boil then remove from heat and cool.

Add orange water or orange juice.

Refrigerate.

Serve cold.

Note: Pour 1 can of condensed milk into a pot of water. Simmer for 1 hour. Remove and chill.

Serve cream with mixed fruits.

The Ultimate Motivation to Diet or How I Started the "Mooning Experience"!

Here at The Culinary Institute of America we live and breathe healthy, nutritional philosophies. We teach stress management and culinary fundamentals to help our guests stay fit, trim, and healthy.

Well, there was a time when I was a whopping 360 pounds of prime beef. It was the glorious year of 1973, and we decided to attend the American Culinary Federation's Convention in sunny Hawaii.

We boarded a large Boeing 747 and I sat down and tried to close the safety belt. It did not fit, and I had to ask for two extension belts! (Sometime later, I suffered lunch. Afterward I asked the stewardess for the recipe so I could burn it to ensure the chef could never use it again.) We arrived in Honolulu, and I could not get out of my seat; they needed two mechanics and a crane to get me loose. This was the first hint that I needed to lose weight.

The second hint came when we were invited to a formal dinner. The dress code was a Florida tuxedo: white pants, a red sash, a tuxedo shirt and a flower lei. Lacking the formal wear, we went shopping, but nobody had my size. Finally, we found Omar the Tentmaker who sold us a pair of white pants. He also sold me an oversized red banquet tablecloth to use as a sash. Later that evening I dressed, but the pants were so tight that I decided to remove my underwear as they were bulging out like sausages. The table-sized sash fitted perfectly, the shirt was tight and the lei delicious. On I marched to dinner. I tried to sit down very carefully as my pants were stretched to the limit, but I changed my mind and decided to stand in order not to stretch them any further.

Somebody dropped a napkin, and when I bent down to retrieve it, I heard a ripping sound. My pants split open from one side to the other. The president's wife, who was standing behind me, was left looking at my full moon. A little sound, "pft," escaped moving upwards like an Italian fountain. There was silence, then there was laughter. I ended up on the bidet in the ladies powder room (ow!) while the attendant stitched up my pants. Luckily, the oversized sash covered the rough stitches, and I finished the evening without much stress. I guess this was the beginning of the trend called "mooning," which is now practiced all over the world. But that is another story.

The third hint I needed to lose weight came on the way back to Hyde Park. I boarded a small plane nicknamed "Kamikaze" to fly home from Kennedy Airport, where I met my good friend, Wayne, who was also in his "prime." We sat together, our extension belts covering our muscular bodies, and the plane started to roll down the runway, but it suddenly stopped. The captain came up to us and asked us to separate in order to balance the plane. Once we accommodated our captain, the plane took off sluggishly.

Ever since that trip I have been on diets; today my weight is 230 pounds and going down. The moral of the story is eat healthy, eat small portions, exercise, and always watch your weight!

Fish Fritter with Breadstick and Marinated Radishes Appetizer
(4 portions)

Ingredients

1	Shallot (small), diced
4	Mushrooms, diced
Butter	To sauté
To taste	Salt, pepper, and lemon juice
4 oz.	Scallops
3–4 oz.	Heavy cream
6 oz.	Stripped bass, pike, or trout, cubed small
1 tbsp.	Parsley, chopped
6 oz.	Radishes, shredded
To taste	Salt
2–3 tbsp.	Chives, diced
2 slices	Bread, cubed

Marinade

Up to 4 tbsp.	Vinegar
6 tbsp.	Olive oil
To taste	Salt, pepper, and sugar
4 sprigs	Dill

Method

Sauté shallots and mushrooms in butter with salt and pepper.
Chill in refrigerator.
Season scallops with salt and pepper, place in freezer for 30 minutes.
Remove scallops from freezer and place in food processor and puree until fine; slowly add heavy cream until the mixture has a creamy consistency.
Place mixture into a bowl. Fold in fish, shallots, mushrooms, and parsley and refrigerate.
Adjust seasoning.
Cube bread and sauté or deep fry in oil until crisp.
Salt shredded radishes and let them rest for 4 to 5 minutes.
Add vinegar and chives and mix well.
Heat oil and mold the forcement into dumpling fritter with 2 tablespoons.
Place fritter into hot oil and pan fry to a golden color.
Place on marinated radishes.
Sprinkle with croutons.
Decorate with dill and serve.

Mustard Soup with Salmon
(4 portions)

Ingredients

1¼ pt.	Fish broth or chicken broth
3 oz.	White wine
1 sprig	Fresh tarragon
7 oz.	Sour cream
2 tbsp.	Dill, chopped
1 tsp.	Pink peppercorns
4 (3-oz. portions)	Salmon steaks
1 tsp.	Turmeric
To taste	Salt and pepper
4 tbsp.	Mustard
2 oz.	Whole butter

Method

Combine fish broth, white wine, and tarragon and bring to a boil.
Add salmon steaks, remove from heat and poach for 5 minutes.
Remove fish from liquid and keep warm. Remove the tarragon.
Add sour cream and turmeric and reduce the liquid by one-third.
Add mustard and bring to a boil.
Adjust seasoning and fold in butter.
Place fish on a plate, pour mustard soup over it, and decorate with pink peppercorns
Add chopped dill.
Serve with pumpernickel bread.

Spiced Asian Pear Crisp
(6-9 portions)

Ingredients

8	Pears (medium), peeled, cored, thick slices
½ cup	Brown sugar
1 tbsp.	Lemon juice
1 tsp.	Lemon zest, grated
¼ tsp.	Ground ginger
¾ tsp.	Ground cinnamon
¼ tsp.	Ground nutmeg
½ cup	Flour
½ cup	Oatmeal, rolled quick cooking
½ cup	Walnuts or pecans, toasted
½ cup	Granulated sugar
½ tsp.	Salt
4 tbsp.	Cold butter, cubed
2 tbsp.	Cold butter to finish

Method

Preheat oven to 375 degrees F.
Lightly butter or spray a deep 2-quart dish.
Combine pears, brown sugar, lemon juice, zest, ¼ tsp. of cinnamon, and the nutmeg and ginger. Place in the dish.
Combine flour, oatmeal, nuts, ginger, salt, and the remaining cinnamon in a processor. Pulse the machine a few times to roughly combine the mixture. Add 4 tbsp. of butter and process until crumbly. Do not overprocess.
Sprinkle mixture over the pears evenly, and sprinkle with 2 tbsp. of butter and bake until golden brown or pears are tender (about 1 hour).
Serve warm with vanilla ice cream, whipped cream, or curls of cheddar cheese.

Roasted Chicken Breast with Potato Roulade
(4 portions)

Ingredients

Chicken Breast

4	Chicken breasts with skin
To taste	Salt, pepper, and nutmeg
Some	Oil for roasting
4	Savoy cabbage leaves, blanched

Crepe

2 oz.	Flour
1 cup	Milk
2 tbsp.	Melted butter
2	Whole eggs
Some	Salt
1 tspn.	Chopped parsley

Port Wine Sauce

2	Shallots, finely diced
2 tbsp.	Tomato ketchup
1	Potato, grated
1	Garlic clove, mashed
½ cup	Port or red wine
1 cup	Beer
1 small	Green apple, peeled, cored, and diced
To taste	Salt and pepper

Roulade

1 lb.	Mealy potatoes
2	Egg yolks
To taste	Salt, pepper, and nutmeg
1 oz.	Carrots, shredded
1 oz.	Celery, shredded
1½ oz.	Green beans, shredded
1 oz.	Crisp bacon, diced
1 oz.	Fresh pineapple, shredded
2 tbsp.	Chives, finely chopped
2 tbsp.	Parsley, finely chopped
Some	Oil to pan fry

Method

For the chicken

Season chicken breast with salt and pepper and roast at 350 degrees F for 15–20 minutes.
While chicken is roasting, bring a pot of salted water to a boil and blanch the cabbage leaves. Shock in ice water and set aside.

For crepe

Mix flour, milk, eggs, and butter with a touch of salt.
Let the batter rest for ½ hour.
Spray a Teflon pan with oil and make thin crepes.

For roulade

Peel the potatoes, cut into quarters and boil in salted water until tender.
Pour into a sieve and drain.
Puree the potatoes with a masher or ricer and fold in the egg yolks.
Add salt, pepper, and nutmeg.
Place mixture in a bowl, cool slightly, add shredded vegetables, pineapple, and herbs and mix well.
Spread the mixture on the crepes and roll into a roulade and freeze.
When semi-frozen, cut into 1-inch diagonal trenches and sauté in butter until golden.

Sauce

Place the roasting pan used for the chicken on top of the oven.
Remove chicken and keep warm.
Add chopped shallots to the pan and sauté until transparent, about 1 to 2 minutes.
Add tomato ketchup and brown for 2 minutes.
Add mashed garlic, port, and beer and bring to a boil.
Pour into a casserole. Add apples, salt, pepper, and grated potato. Mix well.
Simmer for 4 minutes and puree with immersion blender.
Add chicken breasts to sauce and let them rest 5 minutes before adjusting seasonings.
Heat some butter and toss cabbage leaves, salt, and pepper
Place a cabbage leaf on each plate and top with a chicken breast, the port wine sauce. Garnish with a potato roulade.

Vegetarian Casserole: Sauerkraut Gratin with Pineapple and Potato Cheese Topping and Plum Pepper Sauce
(10 portions)

Ingredients

Gratin

2 lb.	Fresh sauerkraut, rinsed with cold water
2 oz.	Oil
2 oz.	Onions, finely diced
2½ oz.	Water or tea
2 oz.	Pineapple juice
16 oz.	Potato cubes
3 oz.	Fresh pineapple, cubed
3 oz.	Cheese, grated (for topping)

Potato Topping

1 lb.	Potatoes
1 oz.	Oil
4 oz.	Hot milk
3 oz.	Cheese, grated

Sauce

3 oz.	Prunes, pitted
1 tsp.	Tomato ketchup
2 oz.	Vegetable broth or tea
Some	Lemon juice
To taste	Crushed black pepper

Method

For gratin

Preheat oven to 400 degrees F.

Heat oil and sauté onions for 3 minutes. Add sauerkraut, water or tea, pineapple juice, juniper berries, and bay leaf.

Simmer covered for 30 minutes then fold in potatoes and pineapple. Place mixture in a buttered casserole, remove bay leaf and top with potato mixture and sprinkle cheese.

Bake in preheated oven for 30 minutes.

For potato topping

Peel potatoes and cook in salted boiling water until soft.
Drain and steam out the potatoes. Puree the potatoes with butter and milk.
Add cheese.
Add salt and pepper to taste and mix well. Note, if too thick add more broth
or tea.

For sauce

Cut prunes into small cubes and simmer with vegetable broth, ketchup, and
lemon juice for 10 minutes.
Puree with an immersion blender or in a regular blender and season with
black pepper.
If the sauce is too thick, add more vegetable broth or tea. It should be the consistency of maple syrup.
Serve with a cucumber salad: 1 lb. cucumbers, 12 oz. tomatoes, 7 oz. onions, 1
tsp. salt, ½ tsp. pepper, 1 tsp. sugar, 3–4 tbsp. vinegar, 2 tbsp. chopped dill. Peel
cucumber, leaving some green. Slice cucumbers, cube tomatoes, and dice
onions. Season the vegetables with vinegar, sugar, salt, pepper, and oil and
toss. Marinate for 2 hours.

Why I Never Work Friday the 13th

I suppose it began with the unnerving ring of my bedroom telephone, which easily jolted me out of a sound sleep and midway to the floor. I looked out of half-crossed eyes at what should have been a bright, sunlit room. Instead, I found myself in complete darkness. I fumbled for my watch, and a quick squint at its glowing face revealed two very disquieting facts: it was only 4:00 A.M. and it was Friday the 13th.

A small alarm went off inside me, warning me to let the phone ring, but I foolishly ignored it and picked up the receiver. A nervous voice on the other end of the line informed me that the breakfast cook at the restaurant had not shown up, and, to further complicate matters, the dining room was full of people. At 4:00 A.M. on Friday the 13th.

Well, I thought, Friday the 13th has certainly arrived in style. Pulling myself together, I made a few quick phone calls in an attempt to fill the station, and I tried not to think about the effect the number 13 has on me. I dressed quickly and left my apartment, constantly repeating to myself that there was nothing to worry about and everything would be fine. I was feeling better soon. I had almost completely convinced myself things would work themselves out. Naturally, it did not surprise me to find a normally professional, well-functioning kitchen reduced to absolute turmoil and chaos when I arrived.

Amidst all the shouting, cursing, and general confusion, I eventually was able to piece together the story. It seemed that the garde manger somehow had slipped while carrying 10 gallons of Russian dressing and had poured it deftly down the front of the food and beverage manager who, of course, was wearing a new three-piece suit. I thought about telling him that now he was really well-dressed, but as I watched him lurch madly for the throat of the garde manger, I realized that my comment might not be received in quite the same spirit in which it was offered. In an effort not to aggravate the situation further, I expediently re-tired to my office.

Sitting back at my desk, I considered three alternatives. I could stay and face whatever else Friday the 13th might throw at me, or I could go for a long, no, a very long walk in the park. While I pondered a possible getaway scheme, break-fast miraculously passed without so much as a burned strip of bacon. Needless to say, I was surprised but pleased. When lunch came and went like any other, my spirits soared and I felt like I wanted to dance on my desk. Perhaps it was over; perhaps Friday the 13th had finally exhausted itself. Soon, I actually was looking forward to dinner.

I think it was probably the maitre d' frantically hammering on my office door and crying that all hell was breaking loose in the dining room that sobered me up to the sad truth that Friday the 13th was still lurking.

Although pale and agitated, the maitre d' said nothing as he led me into the dining room. When we reached the door he groaned, "Look," and pushed me through the doors. What I saw only can be described as being a cross between a Fellini movie and a comic opera by Gilbert and Sullivan.

In the center of the room a young woman was lying prone on the floor with a man kneeling over her alternately kissing her face and shouting for someone to bring smelling salts. These two principal actors were accompanied by various other guests, many of whom were standing on their chairs pointing at what appeared to be the walls and tables. "There it goes!" one would shout. "Watch it! Catch it" The waiters, normally sedate and relatively unflappable, were running and hopping about wildly like overactive children in response to the guests' cries and anxious gesticulations. Girding up what little strength I had left, I gingerly stepped into this circus atmosphere and wondered aloud if there was still enough daylight for that long walk in the park.

The story of what led to this scene follows. The young woman and the man (our principal actors) were a newlywed couple who apparently had been enjoying their honeymoon to the fullest when it must have occurred to one of them that they still had to eat occasionally. Happily, they found their way to our dining room where everything had gone well until the salad course was brought out and the bride set her fork into it. Suddenly, a large frog leapt out of her bowl and down to the floor, followed by the young woman herself a second later in a dead faint. The groom, quick to act, ran to her side and attempted to revive her. Meanwhile, the other guests and the waiters who witnessed the incident joined in a gallant attempt to apprehend the culpable frog. Finally, a group of particularly adroit waiters worked the frog into a corner, captured it and sealed it in an empty cookie jar.

Soon after the incident, the bride revived and was heard to remark something about going home to mother, and left the dining room in tears. The groom, in an admirably romantic gesture, swore that if anything happened to his bride as a result of this "outrageous occurrence," he would "haul the entire restaurant, myself, and the frog into court." I assume that she recovered because we never hard from him again.

Nevertheless, this story is an excellent illustration of why I still have a strong aversion to Friday the 13th, frogs, and, of course, marriage. Together they make a deadly combination!

Pea Soup with Gravlax

Ingredients

7 oz.	Split peas, soaked in cold water overnight
1	Shallots, finely diced
4 leaves	Mint
4½ oz.	Heavy cream
4 oz.	Sour cream
1	Egg yolk
1 tbsp.	Butter or oil
1½ pt.	Chicken broth
To taste	Salt and pepper
6 oz.	Gravlax (see recipe)

Method

Heat butter or oil. Add shallots and peas and sweat for 5 minutes.
Add broth and cook until the peas are soft.
Puree with an immersion blender.
Mix cream and egg yolk and fold into pea soup.
Bring soup to a boil and add sour cream.
Adjust seasonings.
Garnish with gravlax and a sprig of dill.

Frog Legs Provencal
(4 portions)

Ingredients

16	Frog legs
Some	Flour to dust
2	Garlic cloves, chopped fine
To taste	Black pepper, freshly ground
1 oz.	Butter
¼ cup	Olive oil
3 tbsp.	Shallots, finely chopped
2 tbsp.	Parsley, chopped
4 large	Tomato concasse, cubed
½ cup.	Tomato juice
To taste	Salt, pepper, and sugar
2 tbsp.	Whipped cream

Method

Dry frog legs with a paper towel.
Season with salt and pepper.
Dust with flour.
Heat oil and butter and sauté frogs legs for 5 minutes.
Add shallots and sauté for 1 minute.
Add tomato concasse, tomato juice, and parsley and simmer for 5 minutes.
Remove frog legs and place on a platter.
Reduce tomatoes by half.
Adjust seasoning with salt, pepper, and sugar.
Fold whipped cream into mixture and pour over frog legs.
Serve with a baguette.

Fried Apple Dumpling
(4 portions)

Ingredients

9 oz.	Apples peeled, seeds removed
Juice of ½	Lemon
2 oz.	Butter, melted
2 oz.	Confectionary sugar
Marrow of ½	Vanilla bean
Touch of	Cinnamon
1 oz.	Grated almonds
2 oz.	Breadcrumbs or cake crumbs
4 oz.	Grated almonds, toasted
2	Eggwhites, slightly whipped
8	Fillo leaves brushed with butter

Method

Dice apple fine, sprinkle with lemon juice, cream, butter, sugar, touch of cinnamon, and vanilla-bean marrow.

Mix diced apples, grated almonds, and bread or cake crumbs.

Refrigerate for 30 minutes.

Mold 8 dumplings.

Roll in toasted grated almonds.

Dip in slightly whipped eggwhite.

Fold into fillo leaves and deep fry in a 325 degree F. deep-fat fryer.

Place on absorbent paper.

Dust with confectionary sugar.

Serve with apple cider.

Barbecue Sirloin Steak with Grilled Oysters and Grilled Broccoli
(4 portions)

Ingredients

2 lb.	Top sirloin
1 oz.	Rub (see recipe below)
2 tbsp.	Olive oil
12	Oysters on the half shell with chili sauce (see recipe below)
1 lb.	Broccoli with stems, blanched
Some	Salt, pepper, and crushed coriander seeds

Method

Rub steak with spice mixture and let rest for 5 minutes.
Brush steak with oil and grill over medium heat to the desired level of doneness.
Top oysters with chili sauce and place on grill for 5 to 10 minutes.
Season broccoli with salt, pepper, and coriander.
Spray with oil and place on grill for 5 to 6 minutes.
Slice steak and serve with oysters and broccoli.

Rub for Steak

Ingredients

2 tsp.	Ground chili
2 tsp.	Mace
1 tsp.	Nutmeg
1 tsp.	Salt
1 tsp.	Sugar
1 tsp.	Black pepper
3 tsp.	Onion powder
2 tsp.	Garlic powder
1 tsp.	Dried orange peel

Method

Blend ingredients together. Place in airtight jar and store in the refrigerator.

Chili Sauce for Oysters

Ingredients

3 parts	Tomato ketchup
2 parts	Chili sauce
1 tbsp.	Olive oil
1 tsp.	Horseradish, grated
Some	Worcestershire sauce, Tabasco, and lemon juice

Method

Combine all ingredients and let sit for 1 hour before using.

Roasted Red, Yellow, and Green Pepper Salad with Port Wine Vinaigrette and Hot Goat Cheese
(4 portions)

Ingredients

Vinaigrette

1 cup	Port wine
⅓ cup	Vinegar
2 tbsp.	Shallots, minced
3 tbsp.	Sugar
1 2-inch piece	Cinnamon
¼ tsp.	Nutmeg
6 tbsp.	Olive oil

Salad

1 small	Red pepper
1 small	Yellow pepper
1 small	Green pepper
5 oz.	Mesclun
6 oz.	New York hard goat cheese cut into 4 portions

Method

Combine port, vinegar, sugar, salt, cinnamon, nutmeg, and shallots in a casserole and bring to a boil. Reduce by one-third or to approximately ¾ cup. (This will take about 10 minutes.)

Remove cinnamon and place vinaigrette in a blender. Add oil slowly while blending the other ingredients.

Chill, then adjust seasoning and acidity.

Char the 3 peppers over a high flame; place in a plastic bag.

Let the peppers cool for 5 minutes and removed the blackened skin and seeds under cold running water.

Cut peppers into thin strips.

Combine peppers with vinaigrette and let marinate for 1 hour before serving.

Place cheese on a lightly-oiled pan and warm in 400-degree-F oven.

Serve with salad.

Notes

No Trouble at All

"The reason why worry kills more people than work is that more people worry than work . . ."

Many, many moons ago, people in our profession did not have the luxury of attending a school like The Culinary Institute of America. We had to travel and work in many distant places.

I remember when my friend and I applied for jobs in London in order to learn English, and low and behold, we got them! On a cold, but sunny fall day we boarded the train to Oostend in Belgium and took the ferry across the Channel to Dover. (I got seasick, but that's another story.) We arrived in London's Victoria Station late in the afternoon. (I forgot to mention that we did not speak or understand a single word of English.) By using our hands and feet, the old sign-language procedures, we got the taxi driver to understand where we wanted to go: The Piccadilly Hotel on Oxford Street.

Happily the doorman at the hotel spoke German, which is my native language. He arranged a meeting with the chef, and we were put up in a room at the hotel. We would begin work on Monday. On Sunday morning, we went out to tour the city of London. We visited the Tower and touched the ax with which Mary Stuart was beheaded. We stood in awe of the Imperial Guards and visited the Nelson statue in Trafalgar Square. All of a sudden, nature called me, and the call was urgent!

As I said, my English was in the infant stages. I looked up and there was a sign that read "Ladies." Someone had told me "Laddies" is the English name for guys, so off I went. To my surprise, the bathroom was full of women! Well, I thought different countries, different customs, and I sprinkled. Suddenly I was hit with a broom and the attendant screamed. A British policeman arrived and grabbed me. I had no time to zip up and was whisked away to the police station. Everyone was talking to me, and I could not understand a word they were saying. Finally, a German-speaking constable arrived and asked me *"Na sind sie nun perverse?"* which means "Are you a pervert or mentally deranged?""Well," I said "in my country we are normal, we have *herren* and *damen*" (men and women). He said, "We have the same here: gentlemen and ladies. Laddies is the Scottish term for guys, and I hope that I will never see you there again!" With a very red face I promised that I would learn the English language without delay.

The moral of the story is that languages are an important part of our professional lives, especially in today's global setting. While you are a student, you have the opportunity to learn not only English, but also French, Spanish, Italian, and German. If you choose not to, at least learn the proper word for the latrine!

Scottish Broth
(2½ quarts)

Ingredients

3 lb	Lamb shoulder, boned
3 qt.	Chicken broth
5 oz.	Barley
2 oz.	Onions, diced
1 oz.	Butter
3 oz.	Turnips, cubed
3 oz.	Carrots, cubed
2 oz.	Leeks, cubed
2 oz.	Celery, cubed
Some	Black pepper and salt
1 tbsp.	Parsley, chopped

Method

Place lamb meat and bones into chicken broth. Bring to a boil.
Skim off any impurities.
Simmer for 30 minutes, remove bones, and add barley.
Heat butter in a sauté pan.
Add onions and vegetables and sauté for 5 minutes.
Remove all fat from the surface of broth.
Add vegetables and simmer until meat is tender (approximately 60 minutes).
Remove meat and cut into ½-inch cubes.
Add to broth.
Adjust season with salt and pepper.
Add parsley.
Serve with tomato bread.
Note: To make tomato bread, brush a baguette with tomato ketchup. Sprinkle with cracked black pepper and brush with oil. Grill or toast.

Roast Sirloin of Beef
(approximately 10 portions)

Ingredients

8-9 lbs.	Shell strip of beef
1 tbsp.	Salt
2 tbsp.	Coffee, ground
½ tsp.	Black pepper

Method

Preheat oven to 450 degrees F.

Combine coffee, salt, and pepper and rub into shell strip.

Spray beef with oil and place with fat side down in a roasting pan.

Place into preheated oven.

When oven door is closed, decrease temperature to 400 degrees F and roast for 60 minutes, until internal temperature reaches 128 degrees to 130 degrees.

Let beef rest for 10 minutes before slicing.

Serve with grated horseradish, horseradish sauce, or Yorkshire pudding and peas.

Yorkshire Pudding

Ingredients

6½ oz.	Flour
2 oz.	Kidney fat
⅛ tsp.	Baking powder
12 oz.	Milk
6 oz.	Eggs
To taste	Salt
To taste	Nutmeg
10 oz.	Pork lard or clarified butter

Method

Preheat oven to 400 degrees F.

Sprinkle kidney fat with 1 tbsp. of flour and chop fine by hand or in a food processor.

Mix flour, baking powder, and milk until smooth by hand or with a food processor.

Beat eggs and add to flour mix. Mix well and fold in chopped kidney fat.

Let pudding rest for 1 hour.

In a flat cast-iron pan heat lard or butter until it is smoking hot.

Mix dough again and pour into pan.

Place into preheated oven and bake until brown and crusty, about 15 to 20 minutes.

Remove from oven and cut into 2-inch triangles. Serve with roast beef.

Braised Peas

Ingredients

3½ lb.	Peas, frozen or fresh
8 oz.	Chicken broth or tea
½ oz.	Salt
½ oz.	Sugar
3 oz.	Butter
1 bunch	Bouquet of parsley stems
2 tbsp.	Parsley and chervil, chopped

Method

Bring broth, salt, sugar, half of the butter and parsley stems to a boil.

Add peas and cover. Bring to a boil and simmer for 5 to 10 minutes.

Drain and reduce the broth by half.

Add the rest of the butter and toss peas and finish with herbs.

Plum Pudding (10 portions)

Ingredients

9 oz.	Kidney fat
8 oz.	White bread crumbs
3½ oz.	Brown sugar
12½ oz.	Raisins
3½ oz.	Figs, chopped
2 oz.	Citronet
1 oz.	Flour
⅓ tsp.	Ground nutmeg
½ tsp.	Cinnamon
⅓ tsp.	Ground cloves
⅓ tsp.	Ground mace
⅓ tsp.	Salt
4½ oz.	Milk
3 tbsp.	Grape juice
4½ oz.	Brandy
4	Eggs

Method

Preheat oven to 350 degrees F.
Grind kidney fat through the fine plate of a meat grinder.
Mix well with a wooden spoon until smooth.
Add bread crumbs, sugar, raisins, figs, Citronet, flour, spices, and mix well.
Add milk, grape juice, brandy, and eggs. Mix until smooth.
Cover with a moist cloth and refrigerate for 12 hours.
Place mixture into a 1 ½-qt. pudding mold and fill to approximately 2 inches below the top.
Cover with plastic wrap and a cheesecloth and tie firmly with a string.
Place in a water bath. The mold needs to be submerged ¾ inch. Cover with aluminum foil.
Place in preheated oven and bake for 6 to 8 hours.
Cool and place in refrigerator.
Let the pudding rest for 12 to 14 days then warm in a water bath and unmold.
Serve with vanilla sauce flavored with brandy.

Notes

A Thanksgiving Story

Chefs don't make mistakes. . . . they make new creations

Marcus Apicius, 92 B.C.
Taillevent, 1326
Christoforo de Mesis Bugo, 1549
Louis de Bechamel, 1700
Grimos de la Reyniere, 1780

These great men gave us the basis of our food knowledge, but this knowledge did not include the turkey. This beautiful bird did not become known and loved by anyone other than the Native North Americans until the Pilgrims set foot on American shores in 1620. With the discovery of the tasty wild turkey, a new challenge was born. A challenge chefs such as Auguste Escoffier, Alfred Walterspiel, Paul Bocuse, Tim Ryan (you should watch "Cooking Secrets of the CIA" or "Grilling Maestros" on PBS) John Doherty, Larry Forgione, Alfred Portale, and Dean Fearing have continued to meet and overcome, making and the turkey a special holiday dish.

Early in my learning years, I worked in a large hotel in England where roast turkey was featured prominently on our menu during the Christmas season, mainly to please American tourists. Our kitchen had a coal stove that was over a century old. One day the menu offered "*dindon roti*" (French was in at that time). The roast cook's assistant had prepared the noble bird, carefully massaging it with herbs and seasonings, and he placed it into the oven to roast. He took his time cutting the mirepoix, then opened the oven door to place it into the roasting pan.

For a moment there was silence. This was followed by a scream. Everyone rushed to his aid, thinking he was burned or hurt. Speechless, he pointed to the oven. Everyone looked; spectacles were double-cleaned and eyes strained, but the turkey, roasting pan and all, had vanished. An empty, dark oven stared back at us.

The head chef was informed, and he immediately thought of new ideas for the menu, and assigned an apprentice with a high IQ to take a closer look at the empty oven. When he did, the apprentice discovered that the oven had no bottom! Looking further, he found that the turkey was *stuck* in the chimney below the coal oven. With a great deal of "oohing" and "aahing," the lost turkey was re-covered. It was completely black, and it smelled smoky. The chef dusted off the soot, cut a thin slice and tasted it. He clucked his tongue, made funny eyes, and found it had an excellent smoky flavor.

Hastily, he prepared a light mustard sauce and at lunch the menu read: American Smoked Tom Turkey with Mustard Sauce (a new creation by our chef).

To the delight of our guests, black-smoked turkey became a favorite feature on the menu every Christmas season from that day on.

The moral of the story is never be afraid of a mistake or an accident. Learn from it, use a commonsense approach, and invoke the basic fundamentals of good cooking. You can change your food to satisfy yourself and your guest. Listening, asking questions, and getting involved is of the utmost importance in our learning process; it will help us to understand.

Remember! Chefs don't make mistakes . . . they make new creations.

Coffee-Roasted Turkey

Ingredients

1	Turkey, medium size, approximately 10–12 lb.
2 tbsp.	Coffee, freshly ground
1 tbsp.	Kosher salt
½ tbsp.	Ground black pepper
Some	Oil

Method

Preheat oven to 350 degrees F.

Fill turkey cavity with carrots, celery, parsley stems, and onions, or stuffing of your choice.

Mix coffee, salt, and pepper, and rub into the cavity.

Spray turkey with oil and roast in preheated oven for 3 to 4 hours, or until the internal temperature reaches 160 degrees F. Baste often.

Remove and let the turkey rest for 20 minutes. Carve.

Serve with juniper sauce (see page 44), mashed potatoes, and sautéed Romaine lettuce (see page 42).

Glazed Turkey Livers on Red Cabbage Salad
(10 portions)

Ingredients

2 lb.	Fresh turkey or chicken livers
1½ lb.	Red cabbage
3 tbsp.	Red currant jelly
3 oz.	Orange juice
4 tbsp.	Vinegar
To taste	Salt, pepper, and sugar
3 tbsp.	Olive oil
4 each	Apples
2 oz.	Butter
1 pt.	Chicken stock
2 oz.	Walnuts, crystallized

Method

Clean turkey livers and cut into large cubes and set aside.
Shred red cabbage and add red currant jelly, orange juice, salt, pepper, sugar, and vinegar. Set aside.
Peel and core apples and cut into wedges.
Place 2 tbsp. of butter in a pan and melt.
Add 2 tbsp. of sugar and caramelize.
Add apples and toss until coated with sugar, about 2 to 3 minutes.
Heat oil in a sauté pan.
Sear livers.
Reduce heat and sauté for 2 to 5 minutes.
Remove livers and season with salt. Keep warm.
Pour broth into sauté pan to deglaze.
Reduce broth to syrup consistency and toss with livers.
Place raw red cabbage on a plate.
Top with apples, livers, and walnuts.
Note: Chicken, rabbit, goose, or duck livers can be substituted.

Caramelized Walnuts

Ingredients

½ lb.	Walnuts
1 pt.	Water
3 tbsp.	Sugar

Method

Combine water, sugar, and walnuts.

Bring mixture to a boil and simmer until liquids are evaporated and sugar and nuts caramelize.

Spray a hotel pan with oil, and spread walnut mixture onto pan. Let cool.

Note: For a better effect, deep-fry the walnuts.

Sautéed Romaine Lettuce
(6 portions)

Ingredients

3 leaves	Baby Romaine lettuce cleaned and washed, cut in half lengthwise

Marinade

2 tbsp.	Fresh ginger, grated
1 cup	Light soy sauce
4 tbsp.	Dry while wine
2 heaping tbsp.	Brown sugar
3 tbsp.	Sesame oil

Method

Combine all ingredients and partially emulsify in a blender.

Brush Romaine halves with marinade, spray with oil and sauté for 3 to 5 minutes.

Note: Used marinade for spare ribs, if boiled can be used again for other ribs, also your favorite barbecue sauce could be used for this recipe.

Stuffing
(12 cups)

Ingredients

4 oz. (8 tbsp.)	Unsalted butter or chicken fat
2 cups	Onions, chopped
3 cups	Celery, peeled and chopped
2 cups	Carrots, chopped
2 each	Garlic cloves, minced
⅓ cup	Fresh parsley, chopped
3–4 tbsp.	Fresh sage, chopped
1½ cups	Chicken stock
1 large loaf (about 1 lb.)	Bread (Italian or French, cut into ½-inch cubes and lightly toasted) (about 12 cups)
2 tsp.	Kosher salt, or to taste
¾ tsp.	Ground black pepper, or to taste

Method

In a large, heavy skillet set over high heat, melt the butter. Add the onions, celery, and carrots.

Cook, stirring constantly, until the vegetables begin to brown slightly, about 5 minutes.

Lower the heat to medium-low and continue to cook, stirring frequently, until vegetables are soft and brown, about 15 minutes.

Stir in garlic and herbs and sauté about 1 minute.

Scrape the cooked vegetables into a large bowl.

Pour the chicken stock into the skillet and bring to a boil over high heat.

Scrape the bottom of the pan with a wooden spoon to loosen any brown bits.

Boil chicken broth until reduced by half to concentrate the flavor.

Add the broth to the vegetables along with the toasted bread cubes, salt, and pepper and toss to coat.

Taste the stuffing and adjust the salt and pepper as needed.

Stuff mixture into the turkey or bake in a roasting pan.

Juniper Cream Sauce
(3 cups)

Ingredients

3 tbsp.	Butter
1 cup	Fresh mushrooms, sliced
3 tbsp.	Shallots, finely chopped
1 qt.	Beef gravy or brown sauce
2 cups	Dry white wine
10–20	Juniper berries, crushed and tied in cheesecloth sachet
To taste	Salt and pepper
1 cup	Heavy whipping cream
3 tbsp.	Red currant jelly
2 tbsp.	Gin

Method

Melt butter in a medium saucepan.

Add mushrooms and shallots; cook over medium heat 5 minutes or until tender.

Add beef gravy, wine, and juniper-berry sachet.

Simmer over medium heat until liquid is reduced by half.

Season with salt and pepper to taste.

Meanwhile, in a small mixing bowl, with mixer at medium speed, beat heavy cream until stiff peaks form.

Strain reduced sauce; return to sauce pan.

Stir in red currant jelly and cook over low heat until jelly is dissolved.

Stir in gin.

Remove from heat.

Gently fold in whipped cream

Add salt and pepper to taste.

Salt-Encrusted Turkey
(7 portions)

This is an old method of preparing turkey. The turkey was baked in the village or town ovens while the cook went to Sunday services. The beauty of placing the turkey in a salt crust is that it not only held in all the juices, but the crust also could be sealed and marked, providing a guarantee against tampering.

Ingredients

1	Turkey, medium-sized

Cavity Filling

1 sprig	Rosemary
1	Bay leaf

Mix

4½ lb.	Kosher salt
2 lb.	Flour
5	Egg whites
Some	Water

Method

Preheat oven to 350 degrees F.
Knead salt, flour, egg whites, and water into a dough.
Let dough rest for 30 minutes then roll out on a pastry board until large enough to wrap and enclose the turkey. Place it in a large roaster pan.
Spray with oil.
Place turkey in the middle of the dough and bring up the sides to "wrap" the turkey.
Make sure that the crust is secure and there are no holes. (A little water can be used to patch holes if needed.)
Place the wrapped turkey in preheated oven for 3 to 4 hours.
Remove turkey and let it rest for 20 minutes.
Break the crust open and serve.
Serve with stir-fried vegetables cooked separately.
Note: If turkey is more than 12 lb., increase the amount of salt mixture.

Beer-Cured Turkey

Ingredients

1	Turkey, medium-sized
1 bottle	Dark malt beer
1 tbsp.	Powdered caraway seeds
½ tbsp.	Powdered marjoram
1 heaping tbsp.	Brown sugar
Touch	Salt

Method

Preheat oven to 350 degrees F.

Mix all of the ingredients in a blender.

Using a syringe, inject mixture under the turkey's skin and into the breast and thigh meat.

Let turkey rest for 2 hours or overnight.

Mix 2 tbsp. salt, 1 tbsp. pepper, and 4 tbsp. cornstarch and rub into turkey.

Spray turkey with oil and roast in preheated oven for 3 to 4 hours.

Serve with corn stuffing or warm potato salad and coleslaw.

Baked Goat Cheese with Garden Lettuce, Roasted Figs, Apples, and Toasted Walnuts
(10 appetizer portions)

Ingredients

20 oz./wt.	Marinated goat cheese (see page 48)
1 cup	Dry bread crumbs
1 cup	Finely grated hazelnuts or pecans
15 fl. oz.	Balsamic vinaigrette (see page 49)
2 each	Apples, sliced into thin wedges
10 each	Roasted figs (see chef's notes), halved
To taste	Salt
To taste	Ground black pepper
½ cup	Toasted walnuts (see page 40)
1 tbsn.	Chopped thyme

Method

Drain the goat cheese of excess oil.

Gently dip the marinated goat cheese into the bread crumbs and place on sheet pans.

Chill at least 2 hours and up to overnight.

Salad Assembly

For each portion, bake 2 rounds of cheese in a 450-degree-F oven until lightly browned, about 10 minutes. Let the cheese cool while roasting the figs.

Toss 3 ounces lettuce and 3–4 apple slices with 2 tablespoons of the vinaigrette; season with salt and pepper.

Mound on a chilled plate.

Top with goat cheese rounds, figs, and a few walnuts.

Chef's Notes

To roast figs for this salad, remove the top portion of the stem. Cut in half. Season with salt and pepper.

Place cut side down on an oiled sheetpan.

Sprinkle with some chopped thyme.

Spray with oil and roast in a 400-degree-F oven for 5–10 minutes.

Remove, cool, and place on salad.

Marinated Goat's Cheese
with Herbes de Provence
(10 4-oz. portions)

Ingredients

2½ lb.	Fresh goat's cheese
¼ cup	Herbes de Provence
¾ tsp.	Ground black pepper
10 oz.	Extra virgin olive oil
1 cup	Bread crumbs
1 cup	Hazelnuts, finely ground

Method

Place cheese, herbs, and pepper in a mixing bowl.

Mix well with a paddle until smooth, then shape the cheese mixture into even disks about 3 inches in diameter.

Place in a container.

Pour oil over cheese and marinate in refrigerator overnight.

Remove and drain bread evenly with hazelnut mixture.

Balsamic Vinaigrette
(1 quart)

Ingredients

½ cup	Red wine vinegar
½ cup	Balsamic vinegar
2 tsp.	Mustard (optional)
3 cups	Mild olive oil or canola oil
2 tsp.	Salt
½ tsp.	Ground black pepper
3 tbsp.	Herbs (chives, parsley, tarragon, etc.), minced (optional)
To taste	Sugar
To taste	Pepper

Method

Combine vinegars and mustard.
Whisk in the oil gradually.
Adjust seasoning with salt, pepper, and sugar.
Add the fresh herbs if desired.

Shredded Chicken with Applejack
and Sautéed Apples
(2 portions)

Ingredients

8 oz.	Chicken breast, shredded
1 oz.	Oil
To taste	Salt
To taste	Nutmeg
1 oz.	Applejack
1 tbsp.	Tomato ketchup
½ tsp.	Cornstarch or arrowroot
½ cup.	Chicken stock
1 tbsp.	Red currant jelly
Some	White wine
2 tbsp.	Whipped cream
1 tsp.	Parsley, finely chopped

Method

Heat oil, sear chicken and flame with Applejack.
Remove chicken from pan.
Add ketchup to pan and brown for 1–2 minutes.
Add cornstarch or arrowroot, chicken broth, red currant jelly and white wine.
Bring to a boil.
Add chicken and parsley and fold in whipped cream.
Serve with brown rice pilaf or herbed couscous.

Ingredients

Sautéed Apples

1	Apple, cut into quarters, seeds removed
1 tbsp.	Butter
To taste	Salt and pepper

Method

Heat butter to light brown, sauté apple wedges for 1 minute on each side.
Season with a pinch of salt and ⅛ tsp. of black pepper.

Grilled Pears with Chardonnay

Ingredients

4	Pears, cut into quarters, peeled and seeded
1 cup	Chardonnay
2 tbsp.	Sugar
⅓ stick	Cinnamon
1 tsp.	Lemon juice
1 tsp.	Mint, chopped
2 tbsp.	Olive oil
4 scoops	Chocolate ice cream

Method

Combine Chardonnay, sugar, cinnamon, and lemon juice.

Add pears and marinate for 2 hours or overnight.

Remove pears, reserving marinade, and dry with a paper towel.

Brush with olive oil and grill over high heat just to mark (2 minutes on each side).

Reduce marinade by two-thirds.

Place pears on a platter, coat with marinade, sprinkle with chopped mint and serve with chocolate ice cream.

Supervisory Development

Sometimes I wish that we had a school like The Culinary Institute of America when I began my professional culinary career. It would have helped me grasp the academic and practical aspects of culinary arts much easier. I, however, had to learn it the hard way.

In order to learn and train in my chosen profession, I started to work as chef poissonier in a large and prestigious hotel in London. The kitchen was large and built in the early-19th century. It had a coal stove, a coal cellar, a refrigerator cooled by ice, and, of course, a full brigade. My station was next to the breakfast cook in the front of the stove. Beside me was the potagier. Opposite my station was the saucier, the rottisseur, and the entremetier. The garde manger, hors'doeuvier, fish monger, and bouché where upstairs with the chef's and sous chef's office. Our brigade was a melting pot of nationalities.

The chef would not allow us to smoke cigarettes in or around the kitchen. We had a chef de partie from Finland who had a cigarette hung on his lips all day. Every time the chef came by, he just pulled it into his mouth where it lay wrapped in his curled tongue. While the chef went crazy searching for the smoking culprit, he stood there with his mouth closed. The only sign visible was a little smoke coming out of his ears. As the chef left, out came the cigarette. The fish monger, a Scot, was a vivid ballroom dancer. He practiced his steps with a salmon, which he gently caressed, as his partner

The events of one day taught me how not to handle my supervisory role in the kitchen: The entire kitchen was assigned to prepare a dinner for a high official close to President Kruschev of Russia. For security reasons, some of our cooks were given the day off, so we were short personnel. For days we prepared *mise en place* for the extensive classical Russian dinner.

On the day of the dinner, we all started our shift as usual, but this time we were under the watchful eyes of the MI 16, the British counterpart of our CIA, and, of course, the KGB. That's when the problem started. The entremetier, a German, got his kicks in life by throwing potato peelings into the coal fire. He would then pour old beef fat down the hole in the middle of the rings and then green smoke would exit like the smoke out of Aladdin's lamp, rising upwards. Suddenly there was a loud explosion (bang)! An Austrian sous chef (I guess he was shell-shocked in World War II) shouted "Take cover!" as he jumped behind the stove. The KGB agent thought it was a bomb and grabbed the entremetier. The entremetier's commis came to his defense and attacked the KGB agent. The MI 16 gang, thinking the Russians were in trouble, moved in. By now everybody was involved, the Turkish breakfast cook and the Greek potagier waged battle. In between them, a Chinese helper was yelling in his native language. I, on the other hand, grabbed the French saucier—he had always teased me—and I gently laid him into the broiler. Meanwhile, our Swiss garde manger had it out with the hor's douvier from Sengal. The chef came down just as a shoe was thrown by the breakfast cook. It hit one of the Irish dishwashers behind the ear, and he fainted over the garbage can, which brought all our dishwashers and potwashers into the action.

The chef cried out "What have I done to deserve this! Lord stand by me." (He was a Methodist.) At that moment, he was hit on the chin and tumbled through a door into the dining room where he fell over the table of an unsuspecting couple having lunch. That brought the action to the front of the house, which was under the leadership of the maitre d'hotel. He was from Corsica, and his name was Napoleon. It was World War II all over again!

While this was going on, the Italian roast cook was eating his pasta lunch. The turmoil never affected him as he sat there enjoying his pasta, amidst buckets full with coal, as well as flying pots and pans.

The chef recovered with the help of the sous chef. He then stood on a chair, banged a pot and yelled in a thundering voice, "Stop in the name of the Lord!" I believe I even saw lightning, as he was very religious.

We then cleaned up the kitchen, everyone licked their wounds, and we cooked and served the dinner on time. Our punishment came later when we were all docked one week's salary.

The moral of the story is never lose your temper. Control your emotions and, like my Italian colleague, have pasta because "it's good for the nerves." Finally, listen to your teachers in supervisory development.

Pirozhki with Goat Cheese, Warm Tomato Confit

Ingredients

2 cups	Flour
2	Eggs
½ tsp.	Salt
½ cup	Cold water

Method

Mound flour on a kneading board and make a hole in the center.

Drop eggs into the hole and cut into the flour with a knife.

Add salt and water and knead until firm; then let rest for about 10 minutes—covered with a bowl.

Divide dough in half and roll thin, cut circles with a biscuit cutter.

Place a small amount of filling to one side, fold over and press edges together firmly. Be sure they are well sealed.

Drop into salted boiling water and cook for 3 to 5 minutes—don't crowd the pierogi because they will stick (5 to 6 at a time).

Mixture

1 lb. soft goat cheese

1–2 whole eggs

Fine bread crumbs to thicken

Salt, pepper, and chopped parsley

Serve with a warm tomato confit (see page 59).

My Mother-in-Law's Pirozhki

Ingredients

1 cup	Sour cream
2	Eggs
1 tbsp.	Oil
1 tsp.	Salt
2½ cups	Flour

Method

Beat together the first 4 ingredients.
Add the flour (if too thin) add more flour until the dough forms a soft feel.
Divide in half.
Dust off board and roll out each half into a thin sheet.
Cut circles with a dough cutter approximately 3½–4 inch in diameter.
Follow directions on page 55.

Filling Suggestions

Mashed prunes, mashed potatoes, and cheddar.
Potato sauerkraut, kielbasa, cottage cheese and beets.
Serve with smothered vidalia onions.

Tomato Confit

Ingredients

12	Red tomatoes
4 tbsp.	Sugar
8 tbsp.	Water
2 tbsp.	White vinegar
2 tbsp.	Butter
3	Shallots, finely diced
1 tbsp.	Honey
Some	Salt
Some	Pepper
Juice of ½	Lemon
1 tsp.	Parsley, chopped fine

Method

Blanch tomatoes in boiling salt water for 10–15 seconds.

Remove and shock in ice water, peel, cut in half, remove seeds and pulp and strain through a sieve. Save juice.

Heat sugar and water and cook to a light caramel.

Add vinegar, butter, shallots, honey, lemon juice, and tomato juice and stir well. Add tomato halves.

Add salt and pepper and cover.

Braise in a 350-degree-F oven for 40 minutes or until soft.

Add parsley.

Adjust seasoning and serve with pirozhki.

Barrel-Cured Sauerkraut
(Kvashenaya Kapusta)

Russian families once required whole carloads of cabbage to accommodate their yearly sauerkraut making. Although the process of shredding so many heads of cabbage was laborious, it ensured a constant supply throughout the winter, to be eaten plain, mixed with other vegetables, or added to the inevitable *shchi*. The sauerkraut was put up in large oaken barrels, whose scent permeated the fermenting cabbage. Black currant or cherry leaves were often layered with the cabbage, further contributing to its final flavor. Unfortunately, neither oaken barrels nor black currant leaves are as readily available as they once were, so now we must settle for a glazed crock and a slightly more prosaic sauerkraut. Still, it's good! Try adding spices, such as caraway, bay leaves, cardamom, or peppercorns, to vary the flavor.

Ingredients

2–4 lb.	Heads of white cabbage
4 tbsp.	Coarse or pickling salt

Method

The day before you plan to begin making sauerkraut, remove the cabbage to room temperature and let it sit for 24 hours so that the leaves won't be brittle. When ready to make the sauerkraut, remove the outer leaves of the cabbage, then rinse each head and cut into quarters. Remove the cores and shred the cabbage finely.

Pack the salted cabbage in a large bowl and add the salt, mixing to distribute it evenly. Let stand for about 15 minutes.

Pack the salted cabbage firmly into a 4-gallon crock, pressing down on it with a wooden spoon. Brine will start to form almost immediately.

Place a clean cloth over the top of the cabbage. On top of the cloth place a plate that just fits inside the rim of the crock.

Weight the plate down with a jar filled with water or another heavy weight. The brine should rise about 2 inches above the saucer, thus keeping air from reaching the fermenting cabbage.

Leave the crock at room temperature (about 70 degrees F). Bubbles will form, showing that fermentation is taking place. Each day, remove the cloth and any scum that has appeared on the surface. Rinse the cloth out and replace it, and replace the heavy weight on the plate.

If there seems to be a lack of brine at any time (that is, less than 2 inches above the cabbage), add 1 cup of water in which 2 teaspoons of coarse salt have been dissolved.

The fermentation process will take anywhere from 2 to 6 weeks, depending on the room temperature. When the sauerkraut is done, bubbles will stop rising to the surface even though it is still fermenting. Taste the cabbage, and if it is soured enough for your taste, then it is ready and can be refrigerated (Yield: 2 gallons).

Note: The right amount of salt is important. Too little salt results in a soft sauerkraut; too much salt prevents fermentation. Uneven distribution of salt may result in the growth of yeast with a pinkish color.

The top layer of the sauerkraut may turn brown from exposure to air as the cloth is changed, but this layer may be discarded when the sauerkraut is ready to be refrigerated or eaten.

Catfish in Polish Sauce

Ingredients

4 large filets	Catfish
½ tsp.	Salt
⅓ cup	Vinegar
1 pt.	Chicken broth or tea
3 oz.	Gingerbread
3 tbsp.	Raisins
1 pint	Dark beer
1	Onion
1	Carrot
1 tbsp.	Chopped parsley
2 tbsp.	Butter
2 tbsp.	Flour
1 tsp	Salt
½ cup	Red wine

Method

Soak gingerbread and raisins in ¼ of the beer.

Slice onion into rings. Peel carrot and cube small.

In a flat pot, combine salt, vinegar, and chicken broth and bring to a boil.

Heat butter and sear carrots, onion.

Dust with flour and cook for 2 minutes.

Add beer slowly and mix well to remove lumps.

Add gingerbread and raisins.

Add salt and cook for 15 minutes.

Strain and add red wine and simmer for 5 more minutes.

Adjust seasoning and add chopped parsley.

Place filet of catfish into prepared boiling vinegar broth, cover and poach for 15 minutes. Remove and keep warm.

Arrange catfish on platter. Nappe (coat) with sauce. Serve with boiled potatoes and cabbage.

Note: Carp is used in Poland.

Glazed Pork Roast
(Pieczony Schab)

Apple sauce

Ingredients

1 lb.	Small granny apples
2½ oz.	Sugar
¼ stick	Cinnamon
1 tbsp.	Lemon juice

Roast

Ingredients

3 lb.	Pork loin
1 tsp.	Salt
Touch	Black pepper
10	Cloves

Method

Quarter apples, remove core and seeds.
Place together with sugar, cinnamon, lemon juice, ¾ cup of water into a casserole and cook soft approximately 10 minutes.
Remove cinnamon and strain apples through a food mill.
Preheat oven to 400 degrees F.
Season pork with salt and pepper and lard with cloves.
Place roast into a greased roasting pan fat side up and place in the oven.
Roast for 1¼ hours, then top heavily with applesauce and roast for 30 more minutes.
The applesauce will give the roast a golden glaze.
Remove and rest for 10 minutes.
Slice into thick slices.
Serve with sweet and sour prunes and sauerkraut salad.

Nut and Poppyseed Rolls
(Kolach)

Ingredients

½	Yeast cake
3 tbsp.	Milk
4	Egg yolks
½ lb.	Sweet butter
1 tsp.	Salt
1 cup	Sour cream
4 tbsp.	Sugar
4 cups	Flour

Method

Crumble ½ yeast cake in 3 tbsp. milk and let stand for 10 minutes in a warm place.

Cream ½ lb. sweet butter, 1 tsp. salt, and 4 tbsp. sugar together. Stir in 4 cups flour—alternating with 1 cup sour cream. Knead about 10 minutes.

Place dough in covered container in refrigerator overnight.

Divide dough in 4 parts and roll each part out on floured board to thickness of pie crust.

Spread with the filling and roll. Brush with egg yolks.

Bake in 300 degree oven for 20 to 25 minutes.

Nut filling

Ingredients

½ lb.	Ground walnuts
1 cup	Sugar
¼ tsp.	Salt
1 tsp.	Lemon rind or juice
3	Egg whites, beaten

Method

Combine all of the above ingredients.

Poppyseed Filling

Ingredients

2 cups	Ground poppyseed
1 cup	Sugar
¼ cup	Hot milk
1	Large pat butter
1 tsp.	Vanilla

Method

Combine all of the ingredients.

Charlotte Malakoff
(Sharlotka Malakova)

Ingredients

15	Ladyfingers (approximately)
8 oz.	Unsalted butter
1 cup	Confectioners' sugar
4 oz.	Almonds
1 oz.	Semisweet chocolate
2 cups	Heavy cream
4 tbsp.	Framboise (raspberry brandy)
½ cup	Heavy cream
2 tbsp.	Confectioners' sugar
	Raspberries

Method

Lightly butter a 2-quart charlotte mold. Place a round of waxed paper on the bottom of the mold. Line the mold along the sides with ladyfingers. Set aside. Cream the butter, beat in the confectioners' sugar and continue beating until light. Grind the almonds and grate the chocolate finely. Stir the almonds and chocolate into the butter mixture.

Whip the two cups of heavy cream until it stands in firm peaks, beating in the framboise toward the end.

Gently fold the whipped cream into the butter mixture, making sure that it is well incorporated. Pour into the prepared mold. Cover and chill for at least 2 hours.

Just before serving, whip the ½ cup of heavy cream with the remaining confectioner's sugar until stiff. Unmold the charlotte onto a serving platter, and with the whipped cream decoratively pipe rosettes on top of the dessert.

Serve with frozen raspberries.

Yield 6 to 8 servings.

Notes

The Curse of the Pastry Chef

We arrived at Victorian Station in September on a chilly, foggy, Sherlock Holmesian evening. We had traveled from warm, sunny Spain, so the change in weather did not help the situation in which I found myself.

I hailed a London taxi, and off we went to the Piccadilly Hotel in the heart of the city. Because of my limited knowledge of English, I was assigned to work with the garde manger, a German. My first duty was to assist in the preparation of a large, cold buffet. It was the first time I had worked in a hotel as large as the Piccadilly. The garde manger department was manned by 25 chefs; the hot kitchen had 90; and I did not count how many people worked in the pastry department! Observing how such a large kitchen operated was of great interest to me, so I took a tour of the facilities.

As it happened, the chef patissier was working on the final preparations of a 13-tier wedding cake. He was standing on a ladder when I opened the door to the pastry room and pushed him into the cake! Luckily little harm was done, except I was knocked around a little. That, however, is not the end of the story. The wedding cake is at the center of the tale, and it put me between two giants: the pastry chef and the head chef.

The hotel was to be the venue for a wedding reception for an American heiress and a member of one of the blue-blooded families of Europe with a mile-long name. A swimming pool was built into the ballroom and filled with clear blue water for the event. An island was constructed in the pool and that was to be the home of the spectacular wedding cake.

There was also a gondola and gondolier imported from Italy. The gondolier's function was to row the bride and groom over the waters of the pool while singing O Solo Mio. All this was to be followed by the wedding cake carried by 12 young pastry chefs.

The big day arrived, and I was assigned to serve the grand buffet. Plans changed, however, and I was called to the chef's office. One of the cake bearers had not arrived and I was to take his place, over the strong objection of the pastry chef who said, among other things, that I was clumsy. Well, to make a long story short, the bride and groom preceded us and graciously sailed over the waters, waving to a room filled with distinguished guests. As we followed, I could hear the "ohs" and "ahs" from the crowd. Then it happened.

I stumbled. In the frightening silence the cake swayed. First slowly then faster, this masterpiece plunged into the swimming pool to the screams of 500 voices. Stunned by the impact, I was carried away under the protective custody of the entire grade manger department. Fortunately, the evening was saved since we had made an ice craving of a dwarf holding a token wedding cake in his hand.

I was summoned to the office where the pastry chef was loudly accusing the head chef of paying me off to do this terrible thing to him. For the next nine months the pastry chef would not talk to me. In fact, he left strict orders for me to be barred from entering the pastry department from that day forward.

And so, the curse of the pastry chef has followed me ever since. That's why I am not a chef patissier today and I stick to my cooking. After all, when you drop a carrot, the consequences are not so bad.

Peaks and Valley Vanilla Fruit Sauce
(4 portions)

Ingredients

4	Egg whites
2 oz.	Sugar
1	Vanilla bean (marrow)
3	Egg yolks
1 oz.	Flour
1½ oz.	Heavy cream
1 oz.	Butter
Zest of ½	Lemon, grated

Method

Preheat oven to 450 degrees F.

Combine egg whites and sugar and beat into a meringue.

Combine egg yolks, vanilla, and lemon zest and carefully fold into whipped egg whites.

Grease an oval fireproof cocotte with butter and pour in hot cream. With a large spoon, portion out 3 even dumplings and place them in the cocotte next to each other.

Place dish in preheated oven and bake for 8 to 10 minutes or until the tops of the dumplings are brown.

Dust with confectioners' sugar and serve with vanilla fruit sauce.

Note: For vanilla sauce, melt vanilla ice cream and mix with your choice of fruit or fruit mix.

No Wedding Cake Recipe, Please!
Ginger Bread Pudding and Raspberry Sauce
(25 portions)

Pudding

Ingredients

8 oz.	Butter
4 oz.	Confectioners' sugar
12	Egg yolks or egg whites, whipped to a peak
8 oz.	Gingerbread crumbs
3½ oz.	White breadcrumbs
⅓ tsp.	Ground cinnamon
⅓ tsp.	Ground cloves
2 oz.	Lemon peel, finely chopped
2 tbsp.	Orange peel, finely chopped
3½ oz.	Raisins
Zest of 1	Lemon, grated
4½ oz.	Sugar

Method

Preheat oven to 350–400 degrees F.

Combine confectioners' sugar and butter and whip until creamy.

Quickly whip in the egg yolks. In a separate bowl combine the bread crumbs.
Fold half of the bread crumbs into the egg mixture.

Add spices, orange zest, raisins, and lemon zest.

Fold in whipped egg whites and the remaining breadcrumbs.

Place mixture in individual buttered timbales or into coquettes and place in a water bath in preheated oven. Poach 40–45 minutes.

Remove from oven and let cool for 5 minutes. Unmold or serve in timbale or coquette.

Serve with raspberry sauce (see page 71).

Raspberry Sauce

Ingredients

1 pt.	Red wine
3 lb.	Fresh or frozen raspberries, sugarless and pureed
6 oz. (¾ cup)	Sugar
2 oz. (2 tbsp.)	Honey
Juice of 2	Lemons

Bring to a boil.
Serve hot or cold.

Steamed Yeast Dumplings with Walnut Sauce and Blueberry Compote
(approximately 16 dumplings)

Dumplings

Ingredients

1 lb.	All-purpose flour
1 oz. or 1 package of dry yeast	Yeast (mix with warm milk)
½–1 oz.	Warm milk
3 oz.	Butter
2–2½ oz.	Sugar
2	Eggs
⅛ tsp.	Salt
Zest of 1	Lemon, grated
1 qt.	Milk
1	Vanilla bean, marrow scraped out
3½ oz.	Sugar
3½ oz.	Butter

Method

Place flour into a bowl.

Mix yeast with warm milk, starting with ½ oz. of milk.

Make a well in flour and pour diluted yeast into it. Add 2–2½ oz. sugar, eggs, salt, and zest and mix into a smooth dough.

Let dough rise for about 30 minutes.

Punch down and cut into 2-oz. pieces.

Roll pieces into dumplings and place on a lightly floured cheesecloth.

Cover with cloth and let dumplings rise in a warm place.

Place 1 qt. of milk, the vanilla bean marrow, 3½ oz. sugar, and 3½ oz. butter into a large casserole. Mix well.

Place dumplings next to each other in the milk. Cover and steam for approximately 20 to 30 minutes over low heat.

When ready, pierce dumpling with a needle. If dry, remove and place dumpling on a plate.

Serve with walnut sauce or blueberry compote (recipes follow).

Walnut Sauce

Ingredients

9 oz.	Milk, cold
9 oz.	Heavy cream
2 oz.	Honey
2½ oz.	Sugar
3 oz.	Walnuts, toasted and finely chopped
½ bean	Vanilla bean marrow
3	Egg yolks
½ oz.	Cornstarch

Method

Combine 3 oz. of cold milk, cornstarch, and egg yolks and mix well. Set aside.
Combine rest of milk, cream, vanilla bean marrow, honey, and sugar.
Bring to a boil then strain through a cheesecloth.
Combine milk mixtures and fold in walnuts and bring back to a boil.

Blueberry Compote

Ingredients

1 lb.	Ripe blueberries
2 oz.	Sugar
1	Lemon
1 oz.	Heavy cream (optional)
1 oz.	White wine

Method

Combine all ingredients, bring to a boil then chill.

Philadelphia Cream Cheese Cup
(4 portions)

Ingredients

12 oz.	Cream cheese, softened
2–4 oz.	Milk
2 oz.	Sugar
1 oz.	Vanilla sugar
Zest of 1	Lemon, grated
4–4½ oz.	Pumpernickel bread crumbs
2 oz.	Rum
12 oz.	Applesauce
6 oz.	Red currant jelly

Method

Combine cream cheese, milk, sugar, vanilla sugar, and lemon zest and whip until creamy.

Place into a piping bag and set aside.

Mix bread crumbs with rum and let rest covered for 20 minutes.

Place 1 heaping tsp. of red currant jelly into 4 tall wine glasses.

Alternate cream cheese mixture, applesauce, and bread crumbs.

Finish the glass with a layer of bread crumbs then pipe a ring of cream cheese on top.

Fill center with a dab of red currant jelly.

Chill and serve.

Notes

The Incident

"Your temper is one of your most valuable possessions. Don't lose it."

I like this quotation, and I wish I would have found it many, many years ago. It would have helped me avoid many confrontations, as well as aggravation.

During my professional growing years, I worked as a chef poissonnier, or fish cook for you non-Frenchies. It was a cushy job, and I had a lot of time with which to play. I remember one day in particular. It was 1:30 P.M. on a Wednesday.

The hotel kitchen in which I worked had four sous chefs. One was from Germany, one was Canadian, one was Italian, and one was French. The German sous chef looked like Jesse the Body Ventura, but he had a crew cut and drank a lot of beer. He was never fully there, if you know what I mean. The Canadian sous chef was a true professional. He was understanding and passionate, but heavy on the discipline. The Italian sous chef was great. He was a fireball professionally and with the ladies. He shared many stories, and I liked him the best. The French sous chef was highly motivated. He looked like Pepe le Pew, but he smelled better. He was very high-strung, and his speech sounded nasally. He was the sous chef in charge on the day in question.

I remember his voice that day. In fact, I still dream of it. He suddenly called out *"Enleve troi sole bonne femme."* This means "pick up the ordered Dover sole bonne femme." I yelled, "Hold up. You never ordered it." The sous chef started yelling obscenities, in French of course. I called *"En command"* (order), and I called *"Ca marche"* (fire), and he jumped up and down in front of me and screamed in his nasally tone. All I heard was *"Merde"* (this is something that causes a lot of salmonella as well as other things). I lost my temper and grabbed him, and I set him on the glowing hot range. I had to remove him with a spatula because I need the space to finish a fish dish. The sous chef was taken to the infirmary and the chef called me into his office and said two word: "You're fired."

The moral of the story is loud and clear. Never lose your temper. I would not have lost my cushy job. On the other hand, I might not be where I am today if I had not!

Fillet of Sole Bonne Femme
(4 portions)

Ingredients

4	Dover sole (1–2 lb. each), whole or boned
1 oz. (3 tbsp.)	Shallots, finely chopped
2 oz.	Butter
7 oz.	White wine
7 oz.	Fish or chicken broth
Some	Salt
1 oz.	Beurre manir (see page 79, optional)
3	Egg yolks
2 oz.	Heavy cream
1 oz.	Butter
2 tbsp.	Whipped cream
16	Mushrooms, washed and sliced
2–3 tbsp.	Parsley, chopped

Method

Preheat oven to 400 degrees F.

Prepare Dover sole either as a whole fish or cut into fillets.

Brush a flat casserole with butter and sprinkle with shallots.

Top with fish fillets, add white wine, fish broth, salt, pepper, and mushrooms and bring to a boil.

Cover with a lid or buttered parchment paper and braise for 4–8 minutes.

Remove fish (if whole) and remove fillet from bone and place on a platter.

Reduce fond by ½ to ⅔ and thicken with beurre manir if needed.

Combine heavy cream and egg yolks and temper with some of the hot sauce then fold mixture into sauce. Finish by folding in whipped cream and parsley into the sauce.

Adjust seasonings and pour sauce over fillets. Slightly glaze under broiler.

Note: You can substitute flounder, monkfish, seabass, or your favorite fish. Serve with rice, pasta, or salad.

Beurre Manir

Ingredients

1 oz.	Butter
1–2 oz.	Flour

Method

Mix flour and butter.
Refrigerate.

Smoked Salmon Salad
(4 portions)

Ingredients

16 oz.	Salmon, coarsely chopped
Some	Salt and white pepper
1 oz.	Chili sauce
1 tsp.	Lemon juice
1 tsp.	Mustard
1 oz.	Endive, julienned
1 oz.	Tomato concasse
1 oz.	Green pepper, cubed
1 oz.	Pineapple, cubed
2 oz.	Mayonnaise (or sour cream)
1 tsp.	Fresh dill, chopped

Method

Combine salt, white pepper, chili sauce, mustard, and lemon juice.
Add smoked salmon, endive, tomato, green pepper, and pineapple.
Fold in mayonnaise and divide into 4 equal portions. Place each portion on a Boston lettuce leaf.
Garnish with chopped dill and serve with rye bread croutons.

Steak Diane: A Classical Reminder
(2 portions)

Ingredients

2	Sirloin steaks, butterflied, no fat, 7 oz. each
2 tbsp.	Arrowroot
1½ oz.	Butter (or 2 tbsp. of oil)
To taste	Salt and pepper
2 tbsp.	Dijon mustard
Some	Ketchup
Some	Worcestershire sauce
1 oz.	Brandy
10–20	Green peppercorns, from the can, rinsed and crushed
2 oz.	Red wine
1 oz.	Whipped cream
3 oz.	Demi-glace or brown sauce

Method

Flatten sirloin steaks with a mallet between pieces of plastic wrap until they are thin.

Season with salt and pepper and brush both sides of the steaks with mustard. Dust with arrowroot.

Heat butter or oil and sear steaks on high heat for 2 minutes on each side.

Add brandy and flame.

Remove.

Add crushed green peppercorns and red wine.

Bring to a boil and reduce by two thirds.

Add demi-glace and return to a boil, then remove from fire.

Fold in whipped cream and adjust seasoning.

Coat steaks with sauce and serve with rice pilaf, pasta, or sautéed cubed potatoes.

Scampi Your Style
(2 portions)

Ingredients

8	Scampi or shrimp (16 count)
2 oz.	Butter
½ oz.	Brandy
1 tbsp.	Shallots, chopped
1 tbsp.	Applesauce
1 tbsp.	Curry
1 oz.	Cream
To taste	Salt and pepper
1 tsp.	Parsley, chopped
1 tsp.	Almonds, chopped

Method

Heat butter in a sauté pan.
Add the scampi and sauté 1 to 2 minutes.
Add brandy and flame.
Remove scampi and keep warm.
Add rest of butter and shallots and sauté until transparent.
Add applesauce, curry, and cream.
Stir until thickened and add scampi.
Season with salt and pepper.
Sprinkle with parsley and toasted almonds.
Note: Crystallized walnuts give a very different flavor.
Serve with rice pilaf and sautéed curried pears.

Crystallized Walnuts

Make simple syrup (2 pt. water and 6 tbsp. sugar). Place 16 oz. of nuts into boiling syrup and simmer until liquid has evaporated and nuts caramelize. Spread on a cookie tray and mix with some oil to prevent nuts from sticking. For more crispness, deep-fry nuts in 350 degree F oil for 2 to 3 minutes and chill.

Crepe Suzette

Ingredients

4–6	Crepes
1–2 tbsp.	Sugar
2 oz.	Butter
1 or 2 oz.	Orange juice
½	Lemon, juiced
1 oz.	Grand Marnier
Some	Confectioners' sugar
½ oz.	Brandy

Method

Add butter to a sauté pan.

Add sugar and caramelize then add orange juice.

Add lemon juice and dissolve sugar.

Simmer for 2 minutes, add Grand Marnier.

Place crepes into sauce and fold in half then half again and turn crepes over a few times in sauce.

Flame with brandy.

Arrange crepes on plate and serve with vanilla or chocolate ice cream.

Recipe for crepes, page 100.

One Roast Beef . . . and Hold the Piccadilly, or How Sherlock Holmes and a Roast Beef Sandwich Were Responsible for Me Becoming an American

In my early learning and travel years, I worked in many countries and with many chefs who have been in many faraway places. Countless stories were told over these years. Among them were stories of Sherlock Holmes and Dr. Watson and their travels, and, of course, stories of life in America (The Five Orange Pips) as seen by the Master.

I remember working in the city Holmes is so fond of, London. I was preparing the daily cold buffet when the maitre d'hotel returned the roast beef sandwich served to an American couple, saying they refused this ". . . . !"

I was summoned to deal with the complaint. (Insulted chefs often argued and tempers got hot.) At this point, the head chef decided that nothing was wrong, and, as a vivid follower of Sherlock Holmes, to cool the situation he said, "The secret to success is to learn to accept the impossible and bear the intolerable."

He said it in French, which made it sound even more effective. He followed this with "Les Americans sont faches ils ne sont pas, comme to arte le monde." (The Americans are crazy and not like everybody else.)

For me, however, this was not the end. I wanted to find out why they insulted my roast beef sandwich. So, thinking about the great stories, I used the Master's genius and started to investigate the problem. I searched in many countries for the solution, but I did not find it until I came to the United States. While working in New Rochelle, New York, I found the reason for the complaints. I had ordered a roast beef sandwich in an Irish bar, and to my surprise and amazement, the chef sliced roast beef and more roast beef until there was a full 7 ounces! He put it between 2 slices of rye bread and garnished it with potato salad, coleslaw, a pickle and chips. I couldn't believe it; there it was, an American roast beef sandwich! I felt like Sherlock Holmes successfully finishing a case.

In England, a roast beef sandwich consists of 2 thin slices of white bread, a little mustard spread and a very thin slice of roast beef and garnished with mustard cress.

I hope the unknown American couple will forgive us for doubting their state of mind.

The moral of the story is: read, study, and follow the Master's writing. Reading "The Five Orange Pips" and a roast beef sandwich brought me to America to find my destiny, and as ordered, let me put "the recipe" on the sundial.

My Version of an Open Roast Beef Sandwich
(2 portions)

Ingredients

4 slices	Toast with crust
7 oz.	Cheddar or Chester cheese
2 tsp.	Pale ale
4 slices	Roast beef, sliced thin

Method

Cut cheese into small dice, pour beer on top.
Season with a small pinch of cayenne pepper and a little mustard.
Top toast with roast beef slices.
Melt cheese mixture and pour over roast beef.
Serve immediately.

Scrambled Eggs on Tomato and Rye Bread
(4 portions)

Ingredients

4 slices	Rye bread with caraway seeds
4 slices	Bacon
4 small	Tomatoes
2 tbsp.	Butter
1 tsp.	Mustard
4	Whole eggs
2 tbsp.	Milk or sour cream
½ tsp.	Salt
Some	Black pepper
2 tbsp.	Chives, chopped

Method

Toast rye bread.
Sauté bacon until crisp.
Slice tomatoes into 16 even slices.
Mix 1 tbsp. of butter with mustard and spread over toast.
Top with tomatoes.
Add rest of butter to pan.
Beat eggs with sour cream.
Pour into heated pan, add salt and pepper, and scramble.
Place scrambled eggs on tomato, place an rye bread, decorate with bacon, and sprinkle with chives.

Ham Sandwich with Poached Eggs

Ingredients

4 slices	White bread, toasted
2 tbsp.	Butter
4	Eggs
1 tsp.	Salt
2 tbsp.	Vinegar
8 oz.	Ham, sliced thinly
4 tsp.	Mayonnaise
4 tsp.	Ketchup
Some	Ground black pepper
2 tbsp.	Chervil, chopped

Method

Spread butter on toast.
Bring 2 qts. of water with salt and vinegar to a boil.
Break egg into individual cup.
Slide eggs into simmering water and poach for 3 to 4 minutes.
Remove with a slotted spoon and place on a paper towel to dry.
Mix mayonnaise, ketchup, and black pepper.
Top toast with ham slices and poached eggs.
Cover eggs with ketchup-mayonnaise mixture.
Sprinkle with chives.

Bretzel Roast Beef Sandwich
(2 portions)

Ingredients

2	Bavarian bretzel, sliced in half
2 tbsp.	Mayonnaise
1 tsp.	Roasted garlic
½ tsp.	Horseradish, grated
1 tbsp.	Chives, chopped
1	Tomato, cut into 4 slices
To taste	Salt and black pepper
8 oz.	Roast beef or roast pork, sliced thinly
2	Boston lettuce leaves

Method

Combine mayonnaise, roasted garlic, horseradish and chives.
Spread over bretzel and top with Boston lettuce and tomato slices. Season with salt and pepper.
Top with roast beef and the other bretzel halve.
Serve warm or cold.

Pastrami and Sauerkraut Salad Sandwich
(2 portions)

Ingredients

4 slices	Rye bread, toasted
4 tbsp.	Sauerkraut, drained
⅓ tsp.	Caraway seeds
2 tbsp.	Apple, shredded
1 tsp.	Chives, chopped
1 tbsp.	Olive oil
8 oz.	Warm pastrami, sliced thinly
2 tbsp.	Russian dressing
2 leaves	Bibb lettuce

Method

Combine sauerkraut, caraway, apple, olive oil, and chives.
Mix well.
Spread Russian dressing over toasted bread.
Top with bibb lettuce, sauerkraut salad, and thinly sliced pastrami.
Top sandwich with second bread slice.
Note: For different color and flavor, add 2 shredded radishes to sauerkraut.

The Ghost

Today's hotel and restaurant kitchens are scientifically and efficiently designed, with the goal of saving valuable space. This has taken the charm and, in many ways, the motivation out of the kitchen.

I remember working in a large hotel built in the early 1800s. My culinary knowledge was in its infancy, and I was impressed by the kitchen with its high ceiling, large windows, and bustling activities. A huge coal-fired oven range, shining like silver, was topped with shelves filled with copper pots and pans of all shapes and sizes. Chefs worked all around it. Truly, it was the center of the kitchen.

I started as first commis saucier, proud to be a part of this profession and looking forward to working on this beautiful range. Each side of the kitchen was divided into various stations: poissonier, entremetier, rotisseur, etc. Each station had a chef de partie who directed the daily routine and assignments. My chef de partie liked to rise late; therefore, it was my duty to open the kitchen each day at 4:30 A.M. I had to set up the mise en place for the day, including the chef's breakfast table. It was smooth sailing (or should I say smooth cooking) every day until one day when the ghost appeared.

Starting as always at the crack of dawn, I needed an ice pack on my head and toothpicks to keep my eyes open on this particular day because of a rather hectic party the evening before. The kitchen was quiet, and I could hear water dripping, (it sounded like cannon shots), and a few house mice scuttling around. The crackling of the fire gave the kitchen a mysterious appearance. I set up as usual and had just started to brown the oxtail when, suddenly, through the beautiful, aromatic smoke I saw it. On the other side of the range a large tray of cakes floated freely toward me like a flying carpet in the story of Sinbad and the 40 thieves!

My brain told me to run, but my body would not respond, and I stood glued to the floor. While the tray floated closer and closer, my mind went blank and cold shivers ran up my spine as the oxtail started to burn.

Suddenly, an idea flashed through my brain: "It must be Escoffier, the King of Chefs, Chef of Kings returning from the grave to straighten out my culinary life!" As I pondered this frightening aspiration, a Lilliputian pastry chef appeared around the corner holding a tray full of pastries aloft and saying very calmly, "Your oxtail is burning."

Feeling as though a thousand pounds of rock had fallen from me, I found my tongue and stuttered my thanks, resolving that in the future no more fire water would pass my lips. Plain water would replace it.

Herbal Cream Soup
(4 portions)

Ingredients

1 pt.	Chicken broth
1 pt.	Sour cream
5 oz.	Whole butter
To taste	Salt
3 tbsp.	Chervil, chopped fine
1 tbsp.	Parsley, chopped fine
1 tbsp.	Tarragon, chopped fine
1 tbsp.	Basil, chopped fine
2 tbsp.	Sorrel, chopped fine
¼ cup	Heavy cream, whipped

Method

Combine chicken broth and sour cream and simmer for 3 minutes.
Fold in butter and season with salt.
Stir well with an immersion blender.
Fold in herbs and whipped cream.
Serve immediately.
Additional garnishes: Crisp butter croutons, Titi shrimp, poached oysters.

Beef Roulade
(5 portions)

Ingredients

5 (6–7 oz. each)	Beef, sliced thin
2 oz.	Butter
4 oz.	Ham or lean bacon, julienned
4 oz.	Onions, julienned
1 tbsp.	Mustard
Some	Paprika
4 oz.	Pickles, julienned
To taste	Salt and pepper
1–2 oz.	Oil
8 oz.	Mirepoix (onion, carrot, and celery)
1 tsp.	Tomato paste
1½ tbsp.	Flour
3 oz.	White wine
3 pt.	Brown broth

Method

Preheat oven to 400 degrees F.

Heat butter and sauté ham or bacon and onions for 1 minute. Cool.

Flatten beef slices with mallet; place next to each other and dust with paprika.

Spread mustard evenly over slices, then place bacon, onions, and pickles on the beef and form into rolls and tie.

Season with salt and sear on all sides.

Remove rolls from pan, add mirepoix and brown.

Add beef roulade and tomato paste and brown for 1 minute.

Dust with flour and carefully stir.

Deglaze pan with wine and add broth. Add beef roulade. Bring to a boil.

Cover and place pan in preheated oven and braise for approximately 2 to 2½ hours. Turn roulades over once in awhile and keep warm. Remove string and place in a skillet. Keep warm. Strain sauce and reduce by one-third.

Deglaze skillet and adjust seasoning. Pour over roulades.

Serve with red cabbage (see page 163) and spaetzle (see page 97).

Spaetzle

Ingredients

1 lb.	Flour
Up to 5	Eggs
1–2 oz.	Soda water
⅓ oz.	Salt

Method

Mix together and beat until shiny.
Place into Spaetzle machine and drop into boiling salted water.
Remove and shock in ice water.
Drain and chill.
To reheat, saute in butter.

Ragout of Venison with Buttermilk

Ingredients

2 lb.	Shoulder of venison, without bones and cubed
1 pt.	Buttermilk
1 pt.	Red wine
1 pt.	Water
1 large	Onion, cut in half
5	Garlic cloves, whole and peeled
½ tsp.	Sweet paprika
1	Bay leaf
6	Juniper berries
4	Cloves
1 tsp.	Sugar
2 oz.	Oil
To taste	Salt and pepper
1 tbsp.	Arrowroot

Method

Combine buttermilk, red wine, water, onion, garlic, other seasonings, and sugar.

Add venison, cover, and marinate 3 to 4 days in refrigerator.

Preheat oven to 400 degrees F.

Strain venison, reserving marinade. Remove onion and cube, mash garlic.

Heat oil and sear venison.

Add onions and garlic.

Add marinade, salt, and pepper and bring to a boil.

Cover and braise in preheated oven for approximately 1½ hours.

Thicken sauce with arrowroot diluted with some red wine.

Adjust seasoning. Bring to boil.

Serve with spaetzle or smashed red potatoes.

Crepes with Stilton Cheese
(2 portions)

Ingredients

6	Thin crepes made with salt and chopped parsley
3 oz.	Butter
8–9 oz.	Stilton cheese
Some	Black pepper
2 tbsp	Kirschwasser
½ tsp.	Parsley, chopped
Some	Sweet Hungarian paprika

Method

Combine 2 oz. of softened butter with cheese and set aside.
Heat 1 oz. of butter and melt. Add some Kirschwasser.
Place crepe in pan and fill with Stilton cheese and butter mixture.
Fold crepe into thirds.
Season with salt and pepper.
Flame with remaining Kirschwasser.
Sprinkle crepe with parsley and paprika.
Note: Gorgonzola may be substituted. Serve with Mesclun greens tossed with a vinaigrette.
Crepe recipe on pages 14 and 100.

Basic Crepe Mixture

Ingredients

8 oz.	Eggs
2 oz.	Sugar
8 oz.	Milk
1 pt.	Heavy cream
½ oz.	Oil
Touch	Salt
Touch	Vanilla
Touch	Rum

Method

Combine all ingredients and mix until smooth.
Let batter rest for 1 hour.
Butter or oil crepe pan and bake thin crepes.
Store crepes between parchment paper until use.
Note: For savoury crepe use above recipe without sugar, vanilla, and rum. Add 1 tablespoon chopped parsley.

Apple Schmarrn Bavarian Style
(2 portions)

Ingredients

1 oz.	Flour
3 oz.	Milk
1 touch	Salt
⅓ tsp.	Vanilla sugar
½ tsp.	Grated lemon zest
1 tbsp.	Rum
3	Eggs
1	Apple
10–12	Walnut halves
2 tbsp.	Butter
1 oz.	Confectionary sugar
1 tsp.	sugar

Method

Combine flour, milk, salt, vanilla sugar, lemon zest, a few drops of rum and whip smooth.
Fold in eggs. Mix well.
Peel apple and cut into quarters.
Remove seeds and core.
Slice into ½-inch slices.
Heat butter in a sauté pan (Teflon).
Ladle in batter.
Place into a 450-F-degree oven for 5 minutes or when top is dry.
Flip and bake for a few minutes until golden brown.
Tear with fork.
Dust with confectionary sugar.
Add some butter and caramalize slightly in the oven for about 3 minutes.
Heat sauté pan and add 1 tablespoon butter.
Add sugar and caramalize.
Add apples, caramalize for 2 minutes.
Combine caramalized pancakes and apples and walnuts and toss together.
Dust with powdered sugar.
Note: for walnuts: 1 pt. water; 3 tablespoons of sugar (syrup).
Add walnuts and boil until evaporated and nuts start to caramalize.
Spray with some oil and place on plate to cool.

The Perils of Food or How to Cope with a Culinary Shock

The first classes at The Culinary Institute of America begin with an introduction to culinary arts, math, and food science. We also learned about new food concepts and tastes. However, nothing can truly prepare you for a culinary shock and the after-shock.

Many moons ago, I worked on a ship that was built in 1902. It had no telephones, an old kitchen, and no pot washer. Nobody told me about the wind movement on a ship, so when I threw the garbage overboard, it returned right in my face. This experience taught me to always check everything out before I do something.

We stopped for a couple of days in the Middle East and took some time to explore the terrain. While exploring, we were invited to participate in a native feast. We sat on expensive carpets and soft pillows smoking a water pipe. A large bowl of couscous and all kinds of other food were set in front of us. The eyes of a goat floated on top of the bowl. Apparently the goat was sacrificed for our meal and the eyes were a garnish, which turned out to be a major part of the dish. Since we were guests, my buddy Karl and I were served the eyes, which were considered a delicacy.

Well, let me tell you, it took all my strength to lift the eye up to my mouth. I finally succeeded, but the morsel would not slide down the hatch. It took two more gallons of the honey drink they served to get the specialty to slide down my throat, slowly travel to my stomach, and move onward on the long journey through other body parts. I had a feeling it was watching me until it left. I still sometimes think it never left me and it's still watching.

The moral of the story is: as professional chefs, we need to experience, feel, smell, and taste all foods to train our taste sensations. Even if we never experience it again, our memory certainly will.

P.S. On your next visit, I will serve pickled pigs' ears as an eye-opener.

Moluhija (Sour Grass Soup)
(2 quarts)

Ingredients

2 qt.	Lamb broth
Some	Salt and pepper
12 oz.	Sorrel (sour grass), fresh or frozen, finely chopped
8 oz.	Onion, finely chopped
2 oz.	Garlic, mashed
2 oz.	Olive oil

Method

Bring lamb broth to a boil.
Season with salt and pepper.
In a separate pan heat olive oil and sauté onions and garlic for 5 minutes.
Add sorrel and toss.
Place the mixture in the boiling lamb broth and mix well. Simmer 15 minutes.
Adjust seasoning.
Serve immediately with pita bread.

Couscous Chittra
(10 portions)

Ingredients

4 lb.	Leg of lamb
2 oz.	Olive oil
1 tbsp.	Paprika
⅓ tsp.	Cayenne pepper
1 oz. (3–4)	Garlic cloves, chopped
1 lb.	Tomato concasse
6 oz.	Sweet red peppers, cubed
1 tbsp.	Chervil, chopped
1 tbsp.	Parsley, chopped
1 pt.	Water or tea
2 oz.	Butter

Method

Cut lamb into 1½-oz. cubes.

Heat olive oil in a cast-iron pot.

Sear lamb with paprika and cayenne. Add garlic, tomatoes, and peppers and mix well.

Add herbs and water and simmer covered for 2 hours.

Finish with fresh butter.

Serve with couscous (see page 106).

Couscous
(10 portions)

Ingredients

1 lb.	Couscous
1 qt.	Cold water
2 oz.	Olive oil
1 pt.	Boiling water
Some	Salt and pepper
2 oz.	Butter

Method

Soak couscous in cold water for 5 to 10 minutes.
Strain and place it into a casserole.
Bring water, olive oil, salt, and pepper to a boil.
Pour over couscous and cover.
Let couscous rest for 20 minutes.
Fold in butter.
Note: For extra flavor, you can add dates, figs, or grapes.

Baked Bananas
(4 portions)

Ingredients

1 oz.	Country honey
Zest of 1	Orange
Juice of 1	Orange
Zest and juice of 1	Lemon
3 tbsp.	Dark rum
1 tbsp.	Sugar
1 tbsp.	Banana liquor (optional)
5	Ripe bananas
8	Phyllo dough leaves
1 tbsp.	Butter, melted
1–2 tbsp.	Confectioners' sugar
Approximately 7 oz.	Milk
Some	White and dark chocolate shavings

Method

Preheat oven to 400 degrees F.

Place honey, orange juice and zest, lemon juice and zest, and sugar into a bowl over a hot-water bath.

Warm for 15 minutes.

Add banana liquor, mix well, and remove from heat.

Place 4 bananas into bowl and marinate in the mixture for 20 minutes, turning the bananas once in awhile.

Brush phyllo leaves with melted butter; place second leaf on top, brush with butter.

Place phyllo leaves next to each other on a sheet pan.

Place bananas in the middle of the leaves. Spoon some of the mixture onto the leaves.

Brush with melted butter. Fold phyllo over bananas.

Dust with confectioners' sugar and bake in preheated oven for 5 to 10 minutes or until the phyllo becomes golden.

Puree the fifth banana with milk in a blender.

Place bananas in phyllo in soup plates. Pour pureed banana around them and decorate with chocolate shavings.

Serve immediately.

Le Plongeur
(The Potwasher)

Usually the chef is in the limelight, getting all the credit, but behind every famous chef you will find a *plongeur*. In any kitchen (it may be French, German, Russian, or American), you find this person who cleans the pots and pans. This position is often downplayed in importance; nevertheless, let's face it, without a clean pot you cannot prepare a decent meal!

Although the pot-washing section is usually located in the back, it is a central work area of the kitchen. All pots and pans, roasting and braising containers, and most of the essential utensils are kept there. The man working in this area is called the *plongeur* and, in Europe, he belongs to a highly respected guild of *plongeurs*.

Every *plongeur* has his own secret mixture to clean and shine copper. (I once peeked to see one using a mixture of vinegar, cornstarch, and salt.) He presides over large, steam-operated tanks filled with water, soap, and disinfectant, as well as over all pots, pans, and utensils. Because of this authority, *plongeurs* are held in high esteem and cooks bring them cigarettes, food, beer, and wine. These are referred to as TEA. These little favors are necessary because most cooks have their favorite pots or pans and like to use them whenever possible, which can be a problem in a big kitchen.

When I worked as a chef poissonier in England, the hotel had a full brigade and, of course, two *plongeurs*: Paddy and Karl. In introducing myself, I dropped the names of other *plongeurs* I had known, and we became acquainted.

Paddy, as Irish as they come, looked like a leprechaun and had tasted Irish whiskey all around the world. Big Karl, a husky German ex-wrestler who liked his native beer, also had seen the insides of kitchens in many different countries. Every day, Paddy would arrive at 7:00 A.M. and set up his station, filling the tanks with water and detergent, mixing his cleaning fluids, covering the pot-washing table with a fine linen cloth and arranging fresh flowers on it before getting his TEApot filled. Then he would sit down and read the newspaper, getting up to clean a pot very thoroughly whenever needed. Karl arrived at about 2:00 P.M. and both men would sit discussing the politics of the day, food and sanitation, hotel gossip, and whatever else came to mind. All this time, cooks would come and go, receiving their clean pots, plus the latest news and tips for the ponies.

One day, however, the peace abruptly was shattered, and the strength and power of the *plongeurs* was demonstrated.

A new commis on the sauce station decided to take a shortcut and, rather than give his pot to Paddy or Karl, he threw it through the door into the water-filled basin. Dead silence followed the splash, then a scream as little Paddy appeared in the doorway, water dripping from him. His cigar had lost its shape, and the newspaper melted from his hands as he yelled at the commis, who promptly yelled back. At this point, big Karl loomed up behind Paddy. He reached across and effortlessly lifted the commis up like a bundle of linen and dumped him into the pot sink. The commis got one quick but complete dip before Karl lifted him out again and returned the poor fellow to the kitchen, where he stood in a puddle surrounded by the laughing staff.

Karl and Paddy returned to their wet table and, for the next week or so, the commis had difficulty in getting his pots cleaned. I remember he left shortly afterwards as the pressure continued from the pot room. He is now an executive chef in a large hotel and has, ever since that incident, handled *plongeurs* with extreme caution.

The conclusion of this story is that the *plongeur* has his place in every kitchen and in his way is as important as the chef himself.

Pat's Recipe for Cleaning Copper Pots

Ingredients

1 pt.	Vinegar
8 oz.	Kosher salt
2 tbsp.	Tang powder mix
1	Dish cloth

Method

Combine vinegar, salt, and Tang and let rest for 1 hour.
Wipe solution on copper with a dish cloth and rinse with cold water.

Karl's Recipe to Strengthen the Spirit

Ingredients

1 cup	Brandy (Asbach Uralt)
2–3 tbsp.	Sugar
2	Egg yolks
1 drop	Hot sauce
⅓ tsp.	Lemon zest, grated

Method

Whip brandy, egg yolks, and sugar and add a drop of hot sauce and lemon zest.
Let mixture rest in refrigerator for 30 minutes.

Alternative Recipe

Ingredients

1 pt.	Sauerkraut juice
2 pts.	Orange juice
2 tbsp.	Honey
1 cup	Slivovitz

Method

Combine all ingredients and mix well.
Refrigerate and serve over ice.
Note: Karl swears by it.

Paddie's Onion Soup with Beer Bread

Ingredients

2 medium	Onions
½ tsp.	Paprika
1 tsp.	Cornstarch
1 pt.	Oil for deep frying
2½ qt.	Beef broth
Touch	Salt
Some	Fresh ground black pepper
4 slices	Rye bread with caraway seeds
½ pt.	Red and black Irish beer
2 oz.	Butter, melted
2 tbsp.	Chives, chopped

Method

Preheat oven to 400 degrees F.

Slice onions thin and mix with paprika and cornstarch. Deep fry in oil until golden.

Place on a paper towel to absorb some of the fat. (Do not refrigerate.)

Place in a cast iron pot and add boiling beef broth.

Season with salt and pepper and simmer for 10 minutes.

Cut each slice of rye bread in half and dip into beer. Brush slices with butter and bake in preheated oven until crisp.

Serve onion soup with rye bread croutons and sprinkle with chives.

Note: Leftover beer can be used for Pat's Cold Beer Soup (see page 114).

Pat's Cold Beer Soup

Ingredients

9 oz.	Sugar
Zest of 1	Lemon, grated
Juice of 1	Lemon
4½ oz.	Blond raisins
4½ oz.	Dark raisins
6 tbsp.	Crushed zwieback
⅓ tsp.	Powdered cinnamon
1 qt.	Light beer

Method

Place sugar in a bowl.
Add zest and raisins. Fold in crushed zwieback, cinnamon, and lemon juice.
Stir in beer.
Fill soup crocks and refrigerate for 60 minutes.
Decorate with mint sprig.

Bavarian Meatloaf

Ingredients

14 oz.	Beef, lean meat, cubed—semi-frozen
14 oz.	Pork butt, cubed—semi-frozen
16 oz.	Pork fat back, cubed—chilled
2 tbsp.	Salt
2 tsp.	Onion powder
1 tsp.	Dry mustard
½ tsp.	Ground mace
¼ tsp.	Ground ginger
½ tsp.	Nutmeg
1 tbsp.	Sweet paprika
½ tsp.	Ground black pepper
8 oz.	Ice, crushed
1 oz.	Butter

Method

Preheat oven to 400 degrees F.
Grind fatback through fine plate of a meat grinder.
Combine meats and seasonings. Grind through a fine plate.
Mix ground meat and ground fat until smooth. (Use paddle.)
Grease a mold with butter, fill with mixture, score the top into diamonds.
Bake in preheated oven for approximately 1 hour or until the internal temperature reaches 155 degree F.
Note: Can be served hot with potato salad and/or sautéed with fried eggs and home-fried potatoes.

Venison Ragout with Lingonberry Pancakes
(4 portions)

Ingredients

1	Carrot
3 oz.	Celery root
2	Onions
2 lb.	Venison shoulder, or breast, cubed
1	Lemon peel, small piece
2	Garlic cloves
6	Peppercorns
6	Juniper berries
1	Bay leaf
1	Garlic clove
Some	Oil
1 tbsp.	Tomato paste (or 3 tbsp. ketchup)
To taste	Salt and pepper
6–7 oz.	Red wine
1 pt.	Chicken broth or water
1 tbsp.	Butter
3 oz.	Mushrooms
1 tbsp.	Red currant jelly
1 tbsp.	Lemon juice

Method

Clean carrots, celery, and onions and cut into cubes (mirepoix).
Cut meat into 1–2-inch cubes.
Make sachet from lemon peel, garlic cloves, peppercorns, juniper berries, and bay leaf.
Heat oil in a pan and sear meat and mirepoix, tomato paste, salt, and pepper.
Add red-wine, broth, and sachet and simmer for 20 minutes in a covered pot.
Remove sachet and simmer for 45 to 50 minutes or until meat is soft.
Remove meat.
In a separate pan, sauté mushroom in butter.
Puree sauce with a burrstick (immersion blender).
Add red currant jelly and lemon juice and mix with burrstick.
Add meat and mushrooms, adjust seasoning.
Serve with pancake and Boston lettuce, sour cream dressing.

Lingonberry Pancakes

Ingredients

4 tbsp.	Flour
1	Whole egg
5–6 oz.	Milk
1	Egg yolk
1 tbsp.	Butter, melted
5 oz.	Lingonberries

Method

Preheat oven to 350–400 degrees F.

Combine flour, egg, egg yolks, and milk and mix well.

Fold in melted butter.

Let batter rest for 20 minutes.

Heat some butter or oil in a Teflon sauté pan.

Add batter to pan until it is about ⅓-inch thick. Sprinkle with lingonberries and bake in preheated oven for a few minutes until batter is firm.

Tear with fork into pieces.

Return back into the oven to brown lightly

Surround pancakes with venison stew.

Pheasant on Sauerkraut
(4 portions)

Pheasant

Ingredients

2	Young pheasants
To taste	Salt and pepper
3 oz.	Fat back or pig caul (optional)
2 oz.	Butter/Oil

Method

Preheat oven to 400 degrees F.

Rinse pheasant well and dry.

Cover with thinly sliced fatback or pig caul, then truss.

Season with salt and pepper.

Heat butter/oil in a roasting pan.

Add pheasant and roast in preheated oven for 30 minutes.

Reduce heat to 300 degrees F and roast for and additional 10–15 minutes (basting often) or until the pheasant's internal temperature reaches 165 degrees F.

Sauerkraut

Ingredients

1½ lb.	Sauerkraut, rinsed
2	Onions, medium
1	Garlic clove
3 oz.	Bacon
1 tbsp.	Chicken fat or oil
1	Bay leaf
5	Juniper berries
½ pt.	Chicken stock
½ pt.	Dry white wine
1	Bouquet garni (parsley stems and thyme)
1	Mealy potato peeled and cubed
1	Apple, peeled, cored, and cubed
To taste	Salt and pepper

Method

Rinse sauerkraut with cold water.

Chop onion and garlic.

Dice bacon and sauté in a casserole.

Add onion and garlic and cook for 2 minutes.

Add onion, garlic and bacon to sauerkraut, juniper berries and bay leaf.

Season with salt and pepper.

Add white wine and chicken stock, bouquet garni, cubed apple, cubed potato.

Cover and braise for 1½ hours.

Place sauerkraut on a plate and remove the bouquet garni and bay leaf.

Cut pheasant in half, remove back bone, and place on top of sauerkraut.

Serve with potato dumpling or mashed potatoes or sautéed sliced matzo balls.

Homemade Sweet Mustard

Ingredients

9 oz.	Brown sugar
9 oz.	Yellow mustard flour
4½ oz.	Green mustard flour
1½ pt.	Vinegar
1½ pt.	Water
⅓ tsp.	Salt

Method

Combine sugar and mustard flour in a pot. Bring water, vinegar, and salt to a boil and pour over mustard flour mixture.

Mix well and chill.

Note: For change of pace, you may want to add some grated horseradish, chopped chives, dill or parsley.

Pat's Irish Dessert

Ingredients

6–8 small	Hard rolls
1–1½ pt.	Milk
1 tbsp.	Sugar
4 oz.	Strawberry marmalade
4 oz.	Butter
3	Eggs
Touch	Salt

Method

Preheat oven to 400 degrees F.

Cut a silver-dollar-size opening in the tops of the rolls.

Remove some of the inside with a teaspoon and save to top circle of crust.

Combine milk and sugar and warm slightly. Soak rolls in the milk for 5 minutes.

Melt butter in a griswold pan and place rolls in pan.

Fill rolls with marmalade and top with the saved circle of crust.

Place in preheated oven and bake for approximately 30 minutes.

Add eggs to the remaining milk and whip.

Season with salt. Pour egg/milk mixture over rolls and bake an additional 12 minutes.

Serve with whipped cream.

Note: Any type of marmalade can be used.

The Super Breakfast
(Dedicated to All Breakfast Cooks)

Darkness. The alarm clock says 3:00 A.M. This will, I am sure, bring back memories to all you breakfast cooks. It does for me at least!

I remember the mystique of opening the kitchen: the aroma of stale garbage, the quietness, the dripping of water, and the unlocking of all those doors and refrigerators! How I hated unlocking all those doors!

I especially remember one Monday morning. After completing my unlocking tour, I got the *mise en place*, which included bacon from the butcher, eggs from the larder, bread from the bakery, and milk and mushrooms from the storeroom. The breakfast chef arrived and gave his assignments. In addition to our other jobs, we had to break 1,500 eggs to serve a breakfast for 500 businessmen. The menu was orange juice, scrambled eggs, black smoked ham, grilled mushrooms, parsley butter, croissants, coffee, and tea. Everything went as scheduled. The bacon was cooked, the mushrooms were grilled, and the eggs were broken.

On the chef's command, we scrambled the eggs in large frying pans and stored them in big casseroles ready for transport. All food items had to be sent to the banquet kitchen by manual dumbwaiter. The first half of the eggs went upstairs smoothly. The second batch went up and got stuck halfway! The entire breakfast crew tried to overcome the problem. That's when the pastry chef came by and announced that he would correct the problem and he pulled the ropes of the dumbwaiter. The sudden jerk made the pot tip over and all the eggs tumbled down the elevator shaft and onto the pastry chef! It was the first time I had ever seen a yellowed and scrambled chef. He looked like a large petit four.

The banquet manager was told to stall the service, and the chef called the breakfast chef of a neighboring hotel to purchase eggs. A waiter with the facial expression and behavior of a funeral director was dispatched to explain the situation to the hosts. Then we started breaking eggs, again!

The eggs were served with only a slight delay, and the waiter did a surprisingly fantastic public relations job. He told the guests there had been an explosion in the kitchen that had smothered the chefs with eggs and bacon. This story resulted in many get-well cards and flowers, which, of course, we gave to the pastry chef, the only real casualty!

Always remember,
To make a mistake is human
To stumble is commonplace,
To be able to laugh at yourself is maturity.
The game is afoot.

The Beginning of the Day
(4 portions)

Ingredients

4 slices	Rye bread, toasted
1 stick	Herbal butter (1 stick softened butter mixed with 1 Tbsp. herbs, and 1 tsp. lemon juice), cold
2 tbsp.	Butter
7 oz.	Chantrelles, cepes, and lobster mushrooms
4 slices	Bacon, chopped
4 tbsp.	Red onion, chopped
4 tsp.	Lingonberries
4 slices	Swiss cheese

Method

Toast bread and spread with herbal butter.

Heat plain butter. Add bacon and sauté until crisp. Add chopped onion and sauté for 2 more minutes.

Add mushrooms and sauté for 3 to 4 minutes. Season with salt and pepper.

Top toast with mushrooms and Swiss cheese and decorate with lingonberries. Garnish with watercress.

Wisconsin Breakfast Burger
(4 portions)

Ingredients

16 oz.	Ground meat (beef, chicken, or turkey)
2 slices	Toasted bread
1	Whole egg
1 tbsp.	Shallots, chopped
1 tbsp.	Parsley, chopped
1 tbsp.	Olives, chopped
Some	Salt and pepper
4 (thick) slices	Munster cheese
4 slices	Bacon dipped in boiling salt water
2 tbsp.	Oil
4 (thick) slices	Tomato
1 large	Onion, sliced thin
4	Eggs, fried
4 slices	Rye bread with caraway seeds, toasted

Method

Cube white bread and combine with whole egg. Mix well.
Let mixture rest for 2 minutes and add to ground meat. Mix well.
Add chopped shallots, olives and herb seasoning with salt and pepper.
Form burger mix into 4 equal balls, cut each ball in half and flatten into 2 pieces. Top with cheese and the second patty.
Press together and surround with blanched bacon slice.
Heat oil and sauté burger to desired doneness.
Remove from pan.
Add sliced onion and sauté for 4 minutes.
Top burger with tomato slice and onions.
Serve with fried eggs on rye toast.

Potato Omelet with Smoked Fish
(4 portions)

Ingredients

1½ lb.	Firm Yukon gold potatoes
8 oz.	Olive oil
1	Lemon
2	Garlic cloves
5 oz.	Yogurt
To taste	Salt, pepper, and sugar
8	Large eggs, beaten
8 oz.	Smoked trout, without skin and cubed
2 tbsp.	Parsley, chopped
Zest and juice of 1	Lemon

Method

Preheat oven to 400 degrees F.

Wash potatoes and peel, cut into thin slices with food processor or mandolin.

Place on paper towel and dry.

Place olive oil in a cast-iron casserole and fry potatoes until golden brown (approximately 10 minutes). Remove potatoes and place on absorbent paper.

Grate lemon zest, then juice lemon.

Press garlic through garlic press.

Combine yogurt, lemon juice, and half of the garlic and mix well.

Beat eggs in a bowl.

Season with salt and pepper.

Add lemon zest and rest of garlic.

Place potatoes in a buttered cast iron casserole.

Top with the fish and sprinkle with herbs.

Pour egg mixture over potatoes and bake in preheated oven for 10 minutes.

Serve with yogurt sauce.

Steak Tartar with Fried Eggs and Rye Toast
(4 portions)

Ingredients

20 oz.	Tenderloin of beef
To taste	Salt and pepper
1 tsp.	Sweet paprika
2 tbsp.	Dijon mustard
3 tbsp.	Oil
4 tbsp.	Pickle juice
Some	Oil to sauté
4	Eggs, fried
4 slices	Rye bread
Some	Butter for toast

Method

Chop or grind beef tenderloin. Add salt, pepper, paprika, mustard, oil, and pickle juice. Mix well with a wooden spoon.
Form 4 patties.
Heat oil and sear ground steaks.
Top tenderloin mixture with fried egg.
Serve with buttered toast.

Scrambled Eggs with Lobster
(4 portions)

Ingredients

2	Lobsters, 1½ lb. each
	Water, for boiling
2 oz.	Butter
8	Eggs
1–2 tbsp.	Whipped cream
2 oz.	Heavy cream
3 tbsp.	White truffle oil
To taste	Salt
1 tbsp.	Chervil, chopped

Method

Boil lobsters in boiling salt water for 8 minutes.

Remove and shock in an ice bath.

Break tail and claw meat loose and cut tail into medallions. Warm in hot butter with claw meat.

Beat eggs. Add 3 oz. heavy cream seasoned with a touch of salt.

Whip in truffle oil.

Heat some butter in a sauté pan and scramble eggs over low heat.

Just before eggs get firm, fold in whipped cream.

Divide eggs onto 4 plates.

Surround with medallions of lobster and decorate with lobster claw.

Sprinkle with chervil and serve with brioche, page 136.

Salmon Tartar on Rösti Potatoes
(4 portions)

Ingredients

4	Large Idaho potatoes, cooked
To taste	Salt and pepper
8 tbsp.	Oil
1 lb.	Raw salmon, boneless and skinless
Juice of ½	Lemon
1 tbsp.	Olive oil
4 tbsp.	Sour cream
2 tbsp.	Chives, chopped
4	Eggs

Method

Peel potatoes and shred into 4 portions.

Heat 2 tbsp. of oil, in a Teflon pan and add 1 shredded potato.

Slightly press potatoes flat and brown golden on each side.

Cube salmon into small pieces.

Mix with salt, pepper, lemon juice, and oil.

Place rösti disc. on a warm plate. Top with 4 oz. of salmon tartar and a dollop of sour cream. Sprinkle with chopped chives.

Serve with fried egg.

Herring Hash with Poached Eggs and Toast
(4 portions)

Ingredients

4	Matjes herring fillets or Fat Bismark herring
1	Red beet
½ tsp.	Salt
2 tbsp.	Red wine vinegar
1	Apple, Granny Smith
3 tbsp.	Olive oil
1 tbsp.	Red wine vinegar (optional)
2 tbsp.	Chives, chopped
To taste	Salt and pepper
2 tbsp.	Sour cream
4	Eggs, poached
4 slices	Pumpernickel bread, cut in half

Method

Soak herring fillets in cold water for 1–2 hours.
Remove all bones and cut into ½-inch pieces.
Cook red beet in salt water with red wine vinegar until tender, about 30 minutes.
Remove.
Shock in ice water. Peel beet and cut into small cubes.
Peel apple, remove core and seeds, and cube into small pieces.
Place all the ingredients, except sour cream, into a bowl and mix. Heat sauté pan, add 2 tablespoons butter, and heat hash.
Place on a platter and top with sour cream.
Sprinkle with chives and top with 4 minute-poached egg.
Butter bread, cut into triangles and surround herring hash.

Gravlax with Fried Eggs and Mustard Sauce

Ingredients

Gravlax

4½ lb.	Salmon fillets, boneless and skinless
3 tbsp.	Coarse ground black pepper
½ cup	Kosher salt
1½ oz.	Sugar
2 tbsp.	Brandy
2 tbsp.	Dry sherry
1 tbsp.	Dried dill
8 tbsp.	Fresh dill, finely chopped

Method

Combine salt, sugar, pepper, and dried dill.

Sprinkle brandy and sherry over salmon.

Rub salt mixture into fish on both sides.

Press fresh dill on both sides of the fillet.

Wrap fillet tightly in plastic wrap and set in a stainless steel or porcelain dish and refrigerate.

Marinate in refrigerator for 3 days, turning twice. (For better texture, put a slight weight on top of the fish.)

Remove plastic wrap after 3 days. Scrape off salt and dill and rewrap salmon in new plastic wrap and refrigerate before slicing.

Ingredients

Mustard Sauce

3 tbsp.	Sweet honey-mustard
1 tbsp.	Gulden's mustard
2 tbsp.	Coarse mustard
¾–1 oz.	Vinegar
1–1½ oz.	Water
4 tbsp.	Sugar
7 oz.	Oil
2 tbsp.	Olive oil
Some	Salt and pepper
3 tbsp.	Fresh dill, finely chopped

Method

Combine all ingredients except the oils in a blender. Mix well and slowly add oil to emulsify.

Slice salmon thinly and arrange on a plate.

For each serving, slice 3 oz. of gravlax and serve with 2 fried eggs and 1 tbsp. of mustard sauce.

Serve dish with brioche, page 00.

Napoleon of Swiss Cheese
with Tomatoes and Basil
(4 portions)

Ingredients

2 packages	Puff pastry, frozen
6 oz.	Swiss cheese
4 oz.	Smoked Swiss cheese
2	Fresh basil in thin slices

Tomato Sauce

4	Tomatoes
2 tbsp.	Chives, chopped
2 tbsp.	Shallots, finely chopped
3 drops	Tabasco sauce
Some	Ground black pepper

Basil Sauce

1 bunch	Fresh basil, strip leaves
6 oz.	Olive oil
6 oz.	Chicken broth
To taste	Salt and pepper

Method

Defrost puff pastry and bake in a 400-degree-F oven 15 to 20 minutes or until golden brown.
Cut into 4-inch squares and cool.

For tomato sauce

Blanch 2 tomatoes, peel, seed, and dice.
Season with salt and pepper, and shallots and cook for 5 minutes.
Add chives and basil strips.
Cut other 2 tomatoes into wedges, add to sauce and warm.

For basil sauce

Blanch basil leaves in boiling water. Shock in ice water and drain well.
Place chicken stock and basil in a food processor.
Puree and slowly add olive oil, salt, and pepper.

Assembly

Cut Swiss cheese into ⅓-inch slices, the same size as the puff pastry.

Line a baking tray with parchment paper.

Place puff pastry square on it and top with a layer of Swiss cheese.

Season with salt and pepper and sprinkle with basil-leaf strips.

Top with tomato wedges and some tomato sauce.

Top with another square of puff pastry.

Repeat with smoked cheese. Top with basil strips, tomato wedge, and tomato sauce. Finish with puff pastry.

Warm Napoleon in 350-degree-F oven for 2 to 3 minutes.

Place on plate, drizzle with basil sauce and surround with tomato sauce.

Brioche

Ingredients

4½ cups	All-purpose flour
1 package (1 tbsp.)	Active dry yeast
¼ cup	Sugar
½ cup	Lukewarm water
6	Eggs (room temperature)
1 cup (2 sticks)	Unsalted butter, softened and cut into small cubes
To taste	Salt

Egg wash

2 tbsp.	Water
2	Egg whites
Some	Salt

Method

Preheat oven to 400 degrees F.

In a bowl of a mixer with a paddle, combine 1 cup flour, yeast, sugar, and salt.

Add water and beat on medium speed for 3 minutes or until smooth.

Add eggs one at a time.

Beating well, slowly add 2 more cups of flour.

Blend well and add butter slowly.

Beat until incorporated and slowly add 1½ cups flour at low speed, approximately 3 to 4 minutes.

Beat until well blended and creamy. This will become a soft dough.

Remove paddle, cover with a cloth, and let rest for 2 to 3 hours.

Gently deflate with spatula, cover and refrigerate overnight.

Place chilled dough on a floured surface.

Divide into fourths.

Roll each portion into a rope about 12 inches long and 1-inch thick. Divide each rope into 4-inch pieces.

Divide each of these pieces into 1 small piece and 1 large piece.

Roll with your fingers and make 16 large balls and 16 small balls.

Place the large ball in a wide buttered standard muffin tin.

Cut top into an X with scissors. Press small ball into it.

Brush with egg wash.

Let rise in room temperature for 30 minutes.

Place into preheated oven and bake 10 to 15 minutes or until golden in color.

Remove from mold and cool.

Note: Can also be bought in a bakery.

Notes

The Olive

There are all kinds of olives with different tastes, sizes, and colors. They are found in Spain, Italy, Greece, France, and California. These oval morsels are used in cooking and, of course, in drinks. Think of a martini without olives!

During my learning years, I worked in a top-notch hotel with a classical restaurant. The menu, rumor had it, was designed by the great Maitre August Escoffier himself. The kitchen had a brigade with all the classical trimmings. I remember the chef, French, of course, touring the kitchen every day at 10:00 A.M. with five sous chefs at his side. He only spoke French, but his assistants spoke German, Spanish, Polish, Italian, and Swahili. He told them and they told us, the chef de parties.

Then there was the other side—the front of the house. Our chef always addressed them as the birds (penguins). The matrie d' was always properly dressed. The chef treated him badly, but he was a pro. When hotel guests arrived at the restaurant, he greeted them with a deep bow, addressed them loudly by their title and name, making sure everyone could hear who they were, and seated them immediately. He would, however, be very careful to address the women guests by last year's names and only use "madame."

Guests without reservations were greeted with a handshake, and if he felt something in his hand, he heard an imaginary bell ring and rushed to his desk where he had a small mirror and he could see what kind of bill was in his hand. If it were satisfactory, the guests would get a good table. If not, they ended up by the kitchen door or in a poor waiter's station.

The waiters were crusty old souls who wore long white aprons and always stole food from the plates before they were served. It was a show to watch them. One of the garçons (his name was Jim, but they called him Monsieur Sheem) loved to chew olives, and he always stole them from the salads before he served them. Monsieur Sheem was missing his two front teeth and while serving a consommé, an olive pit slipped through the gap and fell into the bouillon while he served it. The man was a pro. The broth was already on the table in front of the guest, so Monsieur Sheem tapped him on the left shoulder. While the unsuspecting guest looked up, Monsieur Sheem removed the soup and pulled the pit out behind the guest's back using his fingers. He then tapped the guest on the left again and placed the consommé on the table. The poor guy didn't know what hit him. Luckily, old Monsieur Sheem wore white gloves (all health inspectors take note). The moral of this tale is that waiters always should wear white gloves and always be aware of olive pits.

Chicken Broth
(10 quarts)

Ingredients

16 qt.	Water
6 lb.	Veal bones
6 lb.	Chicken gizzards (necks and hearts)
1	Chicken
2 oz.	Salt
1 pt.	White wine
1½ lb.	Leeks (white part only), cubed
10 oz.	Carrots, cubed
10 oz.	Celery, cubed
1	Sachet (parsley stems, 2 garlic cloves, 1 bay leaf, and 1 branch of thyme)

Method

Place veal bones, gizzards, and chicken in boiling salt water for 1 to 2 minutes.
Drain and rinse with cold water.
Pour 16 quarts of cold water over blanched items and bring to a boil.
Skim impurities and simmer for 1 hour.
Remove chicken and add cubed vegetables, sachet, salt, and wine.
Simmer for 2 more hours.
Carefully strain broth through a cheesecloth.
Note: The chicken can be used as a garnish or for salads or ragouts.

Meat Broth (Bouillon)
(10 quarts)

Ingredients

15 qt.	Water
4–6 lb.	Beef shank
6 lb.	Beef bones
2 oz.	Salt
5 lb.	Mirepoix (equal parts of cubed carrots, celery, and leeks)
3	Cabbage leaves
1	Onion
6 oz.	Parsley stems or parley root
5	Garlic cloves, crushed

Method

Blanch beef and beef bones in boiling water for 1 to 2 minutes.
Drain and rinse well with cold water.
Cover with 15 qt. of cold water and bring to a boil.
Skim off impurities and simmer.
Add salt after 3 hours or when ready to remove beef.
Cover beef shank with a moist cloth to prevent discoloration.
Cut onion in half and blacken over high heat.
Add onion, vegetables, cabbage leaves, parsley stems, and garlic to broth and simmer for 2 more hours.
Carefully strain through cheesecloth and skim off all fat.
Note: Beef can be used as a garnish for salads and sandwiches.

Garnishes for Beef or Chicken Broth

Royal for Chicken Broth

Ingredients

2 oz.	Cooked chicken breast.
3½ oz.	Heavy cream
3	Eggs
Touch	Nutmeg
Touch	Salt

Method

Puree chicken and cream in a food processor.
Fold in eggs and mix well.
Season with nutmeg and salt.
Place in a buttered mold and bake in a water bath for approximately 20 minutes or until firm.
Refrigerate.
When cold, unmold and cut into cubes or julienne.

Royal for Beef Broth

Ingredients

2 oz.	Tomato paste or tomato ketchup
¼ oz.	Butter
2 tbsp.	Heavy cream
2 tbsp.	Beef broth
3	Whole eggs
To taste	Salt, pepper, and sugar

Method

Prepare as above recipe.

Sour Liver

Ingredients

16 oz.	Calf liver or chicken liver, shredded into thin slices
1½ oz.	Butter
1 small	Onion, diced
2–3 tbsp.	Vinegar
4–6 oz.	Breadcrumbs
2 tbsp.	Parsley, chopped
To taste	Salt and pepper

Method

Heat butter and sauté liver and onions over high heat.
Add vinegar, salt, pepper, and breadcrumbs.
Brown for 2–3 minutes.
Serve with lemon wedge and Boston lettuce, with sour cream dill dressing.
Note: Marjoram can be substituted for chopped parsley.

Liver Sautéed with Peaches
(4 portions)

Ingredients

4 slices (6 oz. each)	Calves or beef liver
1 oz.	Butter
2 tbsp.	Sugar
1 tbsp.	Wine vinegar
1 can	Peaches
1 pt.	Chicken broth
1–2 tbsp.	Red currant jelly
2 oz.	Butter
½ tsp.	Pepper
1 dash	Orange liqueur

Method

Heat 1 oz. of butter in a sauté pan and add sugar.
Caramelize sugar. Add vinegar, peach juice, and broth; reduce by half or until liquid becomes syrupy.
Add red currant jelly.
In another pan heat 2 oz. of butter
Sauté liver on each side for 3 minutes. (Add more butter if needed.) Remove liver from pan.
Sauté peaches on both sides and remove.
Add the peach sauce to the pan and deglaze.
Add a dash of orange liqueur and adjust seasonings.
Arrange liver and peaches on a plate and drizzle with sauce.
Serve with a light curry rice or oriental rice and string beans.

Chicken Liver with Mustard Sauce
(4 portions)

Ingredients

20 oz.	Chicken livers soaked in milk for 2 hours or overnight.
1 tbsp.	Flour
1 tsp.	Mixture of salt, pepper, and sugar
1 tsp.	Sweet paprika
1	Onion, diced
1–2 tbsp.	Butter
1 tbsp.	Yellow mustard
½ pt.	Sour cream
1 tsp.	Thyme or marjoram, chopped fine
⅓ cup	Chicken broth

Method

Drain liver and pat dry. Cut liver into large chunks.
Mix flour, salt, pepper, sugar, and paprika.
Turn liver in this mixture.
Dice onion fine.
Heat butter and sauté liver and onions until brown.
Add mustard, sour cream, broth, and thyme or marjoram.
Bring to a boil.
Season.
Serve with rice, riced potatoes, or home-fried potatoes and a green salad.

Rabbit Legs with Wild Mushrooms
(4 portions)

Ingredients

4	Rabbit legs, 8 oz. each
1	Mirepoix (1 leek, 1 carrot, 1 onion)
1	Celery stalk
8 oz.	Mushrooms, chantrelles, cepes, or shitakes
3 tbsp.	Oil
Some	Salt
Some	Pepper
1 tbsp.	Tomato paste or 2 tbsp. tomato ketchup
1	Sachet (1 clove and 1 bay leaf)
8 oz.	Broth
4 oz.	White wine
4 oz.	Red wine
3 oz.	Heavy cream

Method

Rinse rabbit legs and dry well. Dust with flour.
Cube leeks, carrot, onion, and celery.
Clean mushrooms, slice, and sauté with 2 tbsp. oil for approximately 3 minutes.
Season legs with salt and pepper and sear in oil.
Remove legs from pan and add mirepoix. Brown, add tomato paste and brown again. Add sachet, broth, and wines.
Bring sauce to a boil and add legs to liquid.
Simmer covered for 1 hour.
Remove legs and keep warm. Strain the sauce.
Stir in tempered cream and reduce sauce to a consistency of maple syrup.
Add mushrooms and adjust seasonings.
Place sauce on a plate and top with a leg.
Serve with spaetzle (page 97) and sautéed spinach.

Cordon Bleu of Salmon
with Potato Cucumber Ragout
(4 portions)

Salmon

Ingredients

4	Salmon steaks, 8 oz. each, boneless
4 slices	Smoked salmon
2 oz.	Parmesan cheese, grated
4 oz.	Breadcrumbs
2 oz.	Flour
2–3 tbsp.	Milk
1	Whole egg, for egg wash
2 tbsp.	Oil
1 oz.	Butter

Method

Cut a pocket into the salmon steaks. Season steaks with lemon juice, salt, and pepper and fill pockets with smoked salmon.

Dust steaks with flour, dip in egg wash and crumb mixture (Parmesan cheese and bread crumbs).

Heat oil and butter and pan fry salmon steaks.

Potato Cucumber Ragout

Ingredients

1 oz.	Butter
1	Shallot, diced
10 oz.	Cucumber, cubed, peeled, and seeded
10 oz.	Potato cubes, blanched
2 tbsp.	Fresh dill, chopped
3 oz.	Chicken or fish broth
3 oz.	Heavy cream
½ oz.	White wine
Some	Juiced lemon
To taste	Salt and pepper
1	Tomato, blanched, peeled, seeded, and cubed

Method

Heat butter and sauté shallots. Add potatoes, cucumbers, white wine, broth, and cream.

Simmer until potatoes are soft, about 10 to 15 minutes.

Adjust seasonings.

Add dill and tomato.

Spaetzle

Ingredients

1 lb.	Flour
Up to 5	Eggs
2 oz.	Soda water
⅓ oz.	Salt

Method

Mix all ingredients and beat until shiny.
Place into a spaetzle machine and drop into boiling salted water.
Remove and shock in ice water.
Drain and chill.
To reheat, sauté in butter.
For different flavor, add grated gruyere cheese and chopped chives.

Apple Schmarrn Bavarian Style
(2 portions)

Ingredients

1 oz.	Flour
3 oz.	Milk
Touch	Salt
⅓ tsp.	Vanilla sugar
½ tsp.	Lemon zest, grated
1 tbsp.	Rum
3	Eggs
1	Apple
10–12	Walnut halves
2 tbsp.	Butter
1 oz.	Confectioners' sugar
1 tsp.	Granulated sugar

Method

Preheat oven to 450 degrees F.

Combine flour, milk, salt, vanilla sugar, lemon zest, and a few drops of rum and whip until smooth.

Fold in eggs. Mix well.

Peel apple and cut into quarters. Remove seeds and core and slice into ½-inch slices and set aside.

Heat butter in a Teflon sauté pan.

Ladle in batter.

Place into preheated oven for 5 minutes or until the top is dry.

Flip and bake for a few more minutes until golden brown.

Tear the pancake with a fork.

Dust with confectioners' sugar.

Add some butter and slightly caramelize in the oven for about 3 minutes.

Heat sauté pan and add 1 tbsp. butter.

Add sugar and caramelize.

Add apples, caramelize for 2 minutes.

Combine caramelized pancakes and apples and walnuts and toss together.

Dust with powdered sugar.

Note: for walnuts: 1 pt. water; 3 tbsp. of sugar.

Add for walnuts and boil until evaporated and nuts start to caramelize.

Spray with some oil and place on a plate to cool.

Sherlock Holmes, Mrs. Hudson, and the Hudson Valley

Sometimes I wonder if there is a connection between our beautiful Hudson Valley and Mrs. Hudson, the famous landlady of the late Mr. Sherlock Holmes of London, England. As I read about our valley's history, and its open-door policy to visitors from all over the world who come to visit the F.D.R. Library, Vanderbilt Mansion, The Culinary Institute of America, and many other historical sites, I am reminded of Mr. Sherlock Holmes's dwelling at 221B Baker Street, London. It is here, at this intellectual center in the midst of a large city, that Mrs. Hudson, in her role as landlady, had to keep up with all of Mr. Holmes's desirable and undesirable visitors, as Dr. Watson described in "The Dying Detective":

> . . . a long-suffering woman, not only was her first floor flat invaded at all hours by throngs and singulars and often undesirable characters, but her remarkable lodger showed an eccentricity which must have sorely tried her patience. His incredible untidiness, his addiction to music at strange hours, his occasional revolver practice within doors, his weird, often malodorous scientific experiments, and the atmosphere of violence and danger which hung around him made him the worst tenant in London.

As we read this profile of the Master and the description of his dwelling, our valley comes to mind. In our valley, we are the tenants and our environment is threatened by the "throngs and singulars and often undesirable characters." These characters are things such as pollution and criminal activities. Isn't there a connection? I believe there is. It tells us that we, the tenants of this beautiful stretch of land on the Hudson River, need a Mrs. Hudson to help us keep our valley serene, without violence or pollution. We need to keep our farms without pesticides or chemicals, our mountain streams clear, and our lives healthy, happy, and interesting.

This leads us to the inevitable questions: Who is Mrs. Hudson and where is she today? Well, the simple yet complicated answer is that Mrs. Hudson is us! All of us living, studying, farming, or doing business in the Hudson Valley are Mrs. Hudson as well as Sherlock Holmes: Both identities are part of our personalities. Together we are the keepers, or the landladies, of the land, and we can control the untidiness, the guns, the scientific experiments, the atmosphere of violence, our destiny, and even what occurs in our backyards. Today I see violence, racism, pollution, and the littering of our surrounding areas with cigarette butts and disgusting debris. I hear foul language, people talking behind other people's backs, and rumors being spread every day.

Let's put an end to this! Everyone has to get together. Neighbors, students, teachers, administrators, and politicians need to work side by side to make the Hudson Valley a better place. We all need to become a "mensch" and remember: Stupid people talk about other people; interesting people talk about things; brilliant people talk about ideas. Furthermore, control your smoking; have an apple instead!

Grilled Hudson Valley Vegetables

Vegetables

Ingredients

1 medium	Zucchini, sliced in 1-inch thick
2	Carrots, cut on a ½-inch thick bias
1 head	Broccoli, cut into spears
1	Yellow squash, sliced 1-inch thick
1 bunch	Scallions, trimmed
2	Tomato, medium, cut into 1-inch thick slices

Marinade

Ingredients

1 cup	Balsamic vinegar
½ cup	Soy sauce
1 tsp.	Fresh ginger, chopped
1 tsp.	Garlic, chopped
1–2 tbsp.	Brown sugar
4 tbsp.	Sesame oil

Method

Combine all marinade ingredients.

Place all vegetables in an oval dish and pour marinade over vegetables. Let marinate for 1 hour.

Drain vegetables and reserve marinade.

Grill vegetables over high heat for 1 to 2 minutes on each side.

Heat marinade and serve with vegetables.

Serve with grilled French bread and a glass of Hudson Valley Chardonnay.

Red Beet Soup with Celery Dumplings
(4-6 portions)

Soup

Ingredients

2½ pt.	Vegetable broth, tea, or chicken broth
16 oz.	Red beets, peeled and cubed
2–3 tbsp.	Olive oil
Some	Salt, pepper, and sugar
2 tbsp.	Vinegar

Dumplings

Ingredients

4½ oz.	Milk
2 oz.	Butter
4½ oz.	Flour
2	Eggs
3½ oz.	Celery root, cooked and diced coarse
1	Shallot, chopped
⅓ tsp.	Baking powder

Method

For dumplings

Bring milk and butter to a boil.
Add flour and work with a wooden spoon into a dough (*pate a choux*).
Place the *pate a choux* into a cold bowl.
Work in eggs one by one until fully absorbed
Heat oil and sauté shallots, and add with celery root to dough mixture.
Fold in baking powder and mold into oval dumplings with a teaspoon and
cook in salted water for approximately 20 minutes.

For soup

Peel beets and cube.
Heat olive oil and sauté beets for 2 to 3 minutes over high heat.
Add to broth and simmer for 20 to 30 minutes until beets are tender.
Season with salt, pepper, sugar, and vinegar.
Pour into bowls and garnish with dumplings.

Boiled Duck

Ingredients

2 (4–6 lb.)	Tivoli ducks (or any brand)
6 oz.	Madeira wine
2 each	Bay leaves
¾ tsp.	Fresh thyme leaves
¾ tsp.	Juniper berries
1 tsp.	Fresh sage, chopped
1½ gal.	Basic poultry brine (see recipe, page 161)

Method

Trim any excess fat from the ducks.

Combine Madeira, herbs, and spices with the basic brine.

Weigh each duck individually. Using a syringe, inject each duck with brine equal to 10 percent of its weight

Place ducks in deep plastic or stainless steel container and pour enough brine over the ducks to submerge them.

Use a plate or plastic wrap to keep them completely below the surface of the brine.

Cure the ducks under refrigeration for 12 hours.

Rinse the ducks in cold water and place them in a large pot.

Cover with water and bring to a boil. Simmer for approximately 1½ to 2 hours, or until the internal temperature reaches 165 degrees F.

Remove and chill.

Remove breast for salad. Use duck legs for other dishes such as duck confit or other salads.

Note: Tivoli duck is named for a farm in Tivoli, New York.

Pasta Salad with Roasted Shallot Vinaigrette
(10 portions)

Ingredients

½ lb.	Pasta
20 oz.	Mixed bitter greens (such as arugula, frisee, and radicchio), washed and dried
10 oz.	Chanterelles, halved or quartered (any other type of mushroom can be substituted)
2–3 oz.	Olive oil, for sautéing
1 lb.	Boiled duck breast, cut into strips (see recipe, page 157)
1 pt.	Roasted shallot vinaigrette (see recipe, page 159)
To taste	Salt
To taste	Ground black pepper
3 oz.	Gorgonzola cheese, shaved
5 tbsp.	Chives, chopped

Method

Cook the pasta in boiling salted water until al dente. Shock in cold water, drain, and dry. (Toss with oil if cooked in advance.)

Wash and dry the greens then tear or cut into bite-sized pieces. Keep refrigerated until needed.

Salad assembly

For each portion, sauté 1 oz. of mushrooms in 2 tsp. of olive oil until tender.

Add about 2 oz. of cooked pasta and 1½ oz. of duck.

Toss in a sauté pan over high heat until hot.

Add 2 oz. of the mixed greens and 1 oz. of the vinaigrette.

Toss briskly and mound on a warm plate once the ingredients are just warmed through.

Drizzle with an additional ½ oz. of the dressing onto the salad.

Season with salt and pepper and garnish with shaved gorgonzola and ½ tsp. of chives. Garnish with garlic croutons.

Serve while still warm.

Roasted Shallot Vinaigrette

Ingredients

20	Shallots, peeled
1½ cups	Extra virgin olive oil
1 cup	Sherry vinegar
¼ cup	Honey
1 tsp.	Rosemary, chopped
1 tsp.	Thyme, chopped
1 tsp.	Salt (or to taste)
1 tsp.	Cracked black pepper

Method

Spray the shallots with a little oil and roast in a low oven (300 degrees F) until very tender, well-browned, and sweet-smelling.

When cool enough to handle, cut into quarters.

Combine oil, vinegar, and honey and season with salt and pepper.

Emulsify with an immersion blender. Add chopped herbs and shallots.

Adjust seasonings.

Makes one quart.

Pasta Dough
(yields 1½ pounds)

Ingredients

1 lb.	All-purpose or bread flour
6	Eggs
2 tsp.	Salt
2 oz.	Water, as needed

Method

Combine all ingredients in a large bowl and knead the mixture until it is smooth and elastic.

Cover the dough and allow to rest for 1 hour before rolling and shaping.

Basic Poultry Brine

Ingredients

1 lbs.	Salt
12 oz.	Dextrose, honey, or white or light brown sugar
3 tsp.	Garlic powder (optional)
1½ tsp.	Onion powder (optional)
7 oz.	Tinted curing mix (TCM)
3 gal.	Warm water

Method

Stir together the salt, sugar, garlic powder, onion powder, and TCM.
Add the water and stir until the dry ingredients are dissolved.
Cool brine completely.
Note: If TCM is not available, use Kosher salt.

Sautéed Pork Medallions Mid-Hudson
(5 portions)

Ingredients

10	Pork medallions (3 oz. each)
Some	Salt, pepper, and flour
5 oz.	Butter
10	Apples, cut into ½-inch pieces
8 oz.	Chicken broth
1 lb.	Onions, sliced
1 tbsp.	Chives, chopped
1 tsp.	Sweet paprika
1 tbsp.	Cornstarch
3 tbsp.	Whipped cream
	Oil for frying

Method

Dust onion slices with paprika and cornstarch and deep fry until golden brown.

Place on absorbent paper towels and set aside.

Season apples with salt and pepper.

Heat 2 oz. of butter and sauté apple slices.

Remove and keep warm.

Season pork medallions with salt and pepper and dust with flour.

Heat butter and sauté until golden in color or to a pink texture.

Deglaze the pan with broth and reduce broth by two-thirds. Fold in whipped cream and adjust seasonings.

Drizzle sauce over apples, sprinkle with chives and top with pork medallions. Garnish with crisp onions.

Serve with mashed potatoes and red cabbage.

Braised Red Cabbage
(5 portions)

Ingredients

3 oz.	Goose fat or oil
5 oz.	Onion, julienned
2½ lb.	Red cabbage, shredded
Up to 1 oz.	Sugar
½ oz.	Salt
5 oz.	Apples, sliced
2½ tbsp.	Vinegar
1 pt.	Chicken stock or water
1	Sachet (⅓ cinnamon stick, 1 small bay leaf, 1–2 cloves, and 5 crushed peppercorns)
1 tbsp.	Red current jelly
Some	Lemon juice

Method

Heat fat.

Sweat onions and add cabbage.

Cook for 3 minutes and add apples, vinegar, salt, and sachet and bring to a boil.

Cover and braise 35–60 minutes, stirring once in awhile.

Finish with red current jelly and lemon juice.

Note: For garnish, peel apple, remove core, and slice thin. Place neatly into a buttered sauté pan, sprinkle with sugar, and drizzle some wine on top. Braise for 5 minutes.

For Our Vegetarian Friends: Pan-Fried Celery Cutlet in Sesame and Coconut Herbal Sauce
(4 portions)

Celery Cutlets

Ingredients

3 lbs.	Celery root, peeled, cooked al dente
8	Celery cutlets, approximately 4 oz. each
12 oz.	Bread crumbs
3 oz.	Sesame seeds, toasted
3 oz.	Coconut, grated and toasted
1 tbsp.	Hungarian sweet paprika
To taste	Salt and pepper
	Flour, to dust
4	Whole eggs, beaten with some water (egg wash)
	Olive oil, to fry

Method

Peel celery root and cook in salted water until al dente.
Remove and shock in ice water. (Save fond; it can be used for soups or sauces.)
Slice celery roots into 4-oz. cutlets.
Combine bread crumbs, sesame seeds, coconut, paprika, salt, and pepper.
Dust cutlets with flour, dip in egg wash, and bread the cutlets.
Fry in olive oil until golden.

Herbal Sauce

Ingredients

½ cup	Mayonnaise
½ cup	Yogurt
4 tbsp.	Tomato concasse, cubed
2 tbsp.	Red pepper, roasted and cubed
2 tbsp.	Tomato ketchup
1 tbsp.	Parsley, chopped
1 tbsp.	Dill, chopped

Method

Combine all the ingredients and let rest for 1 hour.

Note: This sauce can be used hot or cold.

1776 Wurtenburg Bread Pudding
(4 portions)

Ingredients

20 oz.	Granny Smith apples
4 oz.	Raisins
4 tbsp.	Rum
12 oz.	Brioche

For egg royal

1½ cups	Milk
1 cup	Heavy cream
6	Eggs
2½ oz.	Sugar
2	Vanilla beans
Some	Confectionary sugar to dust

Method

Spray a large fireproof casserole with oil.
Dust with sugar.
Peel apples, decore, cut into wedges, and slice thin.
Mix raisins with rum and add to apples.
Cut brioche into ½-inch slices and place one half on the bottom of the casserole and top with apple mix and finish with rest of brioche.
Combine egg mixture: milk, cream, eggs, sugar, and mix well.
Add the marrow of the vanilla bean and pour over bread and apples.
Place in a 450-degree-F oven and bake for 15 minutes.
Turn oven down to 350-degrees-F and bake for 30 minutes.
Dust with confectionary sugar.
Serve with whipped cream.
Note: If pudding gets too brown, cover with aluminum foil. If no brioche is available, use roll, white, or rye bread.

Notes

The Practical

Remember that there is no substitute for hard work and careful planning. Failing to prepare is preparing to fail.

Never be afraid of a challenge, whether it is personal competition, the Master Chef Test or the second- and fifth-term cooking practicals. I remember some 15 years ago my challenge was the Certified Master Chef Test.

The biggest obstacle I had in the test was American cuisine. I practiced mental mise en place and researched tons of books. I thought of Cornish hens, turkeys, Kansas beef, Mississippi catfish, Nebraska lamb, plum de veau. I thought of chowders, salads, Georgia pork, and jambalaya. I felt confident and ready to kick some proverbial butt.

The day of reckoning came fast, and we walked down the 35 steps to the meatroom. There on the white table lay all the items of which I had thought. I exclaimed "Alleluia! Alleluia! Alleluia! Sonnenschmidt, you're okay!"

Before we were allowed to choose our meats, however, we had to pick a number. I picked number 10, and all of my fellow candidates selected their choices. By the time I was allowed to pick, the only thing left was a duck and a shank of veal.

I never thought of a duck or veal shank. Father Murphy, Roth Hall's residence ghost (that's another story), was on my side that day. He had pity for a poor Lutheran, and he whispered in my ear "roast, you dummy, and emulsify." My culinary brain went into overdrive, and I asked the master chef evaluator if I could have some pork fat. It was granted. I got the fat trimmings from Tony Seta, who, by the way, got the pork loin! I had my eyes set on it. It brought him luck also, he passed the test.

I proceeded to make a forcemeat from the shank and the fat trimmings. I found some pecans, ham, and peaches on the community table, who sung in unison "Georgia on My Mind." I cubed the duck leg meat, caramelized the pecans, poached the peaches, cubed the ham and added all the items to the forcemeat. Then I rolled and stuffed the duck, tied it, and roasted it. The bones were used to make a simple reduction sauce. I named my creation "Father Murphy's Duck, Savannah Style with Deep South Grits and Color Greens."

The judges went bananas, a food term which means they couldn't get their hands and mouths off it. They ate everything and even licked the plate!

Alleluia! Thank you Father Murphy! I passed!

The moral of the story is that when in doubt, fall back on the classical fundamentals of cooking. Never forget shallow poaching, submerged poaching, braising, sautéing, broiling, and roasting—the basic fundamentals. It saved my culinary career.

Onion Soup My Way
(4 portions)

Ingredients

½ oz.	Butter
3–4 oz.	Crisp fried onions
2 tbsp.	Brandy (optional)
1 oz.	White wine
1 pt.	Chicken broth
To taste	Salt
To taste	Pepper
4	Cheese croutons
4 sprigs	Deep-fried parsley
4	Roasted garlic cloves

Method

Heat butter and sweat fried onions for 30 seconds.

Flame with brandy and immediately add white wine and broth. Bring to a boil for 3 minutes.

Season with salt and pepper.

Serve with cheese croutons, roasted garlic, and deep-fried parsley.

Note: Slice onions thin and mix with some flour and sweet Hungarian paprika, then deep-fry crisp.

Deep-fry parsley for 1 minute. Place on an absorbent paper towel to remove some of the oil.

To make cheese croutons, shred 4-oz. piece of Swiss cheese. Place 4 1 oz. mounds of shredded cheese on a hot Teflon pan. Melt and brown on both sides.

Remove and cool.

Place onion soup in a bowl and top with cheese crouton and ½ roasted garlic clove. Finish with deep-fried parsley.

Duck Steaks Twelve Horse Ale
with Sautéed Romaine

Ingredients

4	Duck breasts, 6 oz. each
4	Shallots, finely diced
3 oz.	Butter
3 tbsp.	Tomato ketchup
1 tsp.	Cornstarch
½ can	Genesee Twelve Horse Ale
To taste	Salt, pepper, and Worcestershire sauce
	Whipped or heavy cream
2 tbsp.	Black pepper and salt

Method

Season duck breasts with salt and butter.

Heat butter and sauté the duck for 5 minutes on each side.

Remove from pan and keep warm.

Add more butter to pan and sauté shallots.

Add ketchup and brown.

Dust with cornstarch and brown again.

Add beer. Mix well to remove all lumps and simmer for 5 to 7 minutes.

Season with salt, pepper, and Worcestershire sauce.

Add duck breasts and simmer for 3 minutes or until they reach desired doneness. Remove duck and arrange on a serving dish.

Whip cream and fold in chervil, salt, and pepper. Fold into sauce.

Pour sauce over duck breast.

Serve with sautéed Romaine lettuce and riced potatoes.

Note: This recipe is easier to prepare than Father Murphy's duck.

Fritz's Midnight Sauce

Ingredients

	Meat, game, or fish
1–2 tbsp.	Onions or shallots, chopped
2 tbsp.	Tomato ketchup
½ tsp.	Arrowroot
½ can	Beer
To taste	Salt and pepper

Method

Sauté meat, game, or fish in a pan. Remove from pan.
Add chopped onions or shallots and sauté for 2 minutes.
Add tomato ketchup. Sauté for 1 to 2 minutes to give some color.
Add arrowroot and brown for 1 minute.
Add ½ can of beer (use more if needed).
Mix well and simmer for 5 minutes.
Add salt and pepper and pour over main item.

Variations

For red wine sauce

After onions, add red wine and reduce to sec. Continue with above recipe.

For mustard sauce

Follow the directions in main recipe, but use white wine.

For mushroom sauce

Use the recipe for red wine sauce, but add mushrooms.
Note: Sec means reduce to zero.

Chicken Provencal for Busy People
(2 portions)

Ingredients

2	Chicken breasts, butterflied and pounded
1 oz.	Butter
1 oz.	Gin
1 oz.	Bacon, diced
2	Garlic cloves, mashed
1 oz.	Shallot, diced
Some	Oregano and rosemary, finely chopped
To taste	Salt, pepper, and sugar
1 tbsp.	Tomato ketchup
3 oz.	Heavy cream
1 oz.	White wine
2 tbsp.	Tomato concasse (small cubed)

Method

Heat butter, season chicken with salt and pepper, and sauté 1 to 2 minutes on each side on a high fire. Flame with gin.

Remove chicken from pan and reduce fire to medium. Add bacon and sauté until golden.

Add garlic, shallots, herbs, and tomato ketchup, and brown for 1 minute.

Add white wine.

Add cream.

Reduce to a syrup consistency.

Add tomato concasse and pour sauce over chicken.

Sprinkle with chopped parsley.

Serve with rice or buttered parsley potatoes.

Green Bean Salad

Ingredients

1 lb.	Green beans, cleaned
1	Red onion, sliced
1 qt.	Salt and water
Some	Basic vinaigrette (oi, vinegar, salt, pepper, and sugar)

Method

Cook beans in salt water until fork tender.
Shock in an ice bath and combine with onions and vinaigrette.
Note: For color, add 3 shredded radishes and 1 tbsp. of bacon bits.

Salad Sampler
(4 portions)

Ingredients

1 lb.	Red cabbage
1 small	Onion
To taste	Salt and pepper, sugar
2 oz.	Vinegar
1½ oz.	Oil
2 oz.	Red current jelly

Method

Shred cabbage. Slice onion.
Blanch in salted vinegar water and drain.
Mix cabbage with vinegar, salt, pepper, and sugar.
Fold in oil and red currant.
Chill.
Note: Finely sliced walnuts can be added.

Ingredients
Cauliflower Roses

1	Head of cauliflower
	Flour and salt
2 qts.	Water
	Herbal dressing

Method

Clean cauliflower, cut into small rosettes and cook in salt, flour, and water until fork tender.
Add herbal dressing and marinate for 2 hours.

Ingredients
Herbal Dressing

3–4 oz.	Consommé or broth
3 tbsp.	Raspberry vinegar
1 tsp.	Mustard
1	Shallot, finely chopped
1 tbsp.	Herbs (chervil, dill, and parsley)
5 tbsp.	Oil

| To taste | Salt, pepper, and sugar |
| Touch | Worcestershire sauce |

Method

Whip all ingredients together well.
Adjust seasoning.

Boston Lettuce with Sour Cream

Ingredients

1 head	Boston lettuce, cleaned and leaves separated

Ingredients

Sour Cream Dressing

5 parts	Sour cream
1 part	Vinegar or lemon juice
To taste	Salt, pepper, sugar, and dill

Method

Mix all dressing ingredients.
Dip lettuce into dressing.

German Potato Salad

Ingredients

3 lbs.	Yukon gold potatoes (or potatoes of your choice)
5 oz.	Onions, finely diced
1 cup	Plain white vinegar
2 cups	Strong chicken or beef broth (you may want to use some chicken base)
Some	Sugar and salt
3 oz.	Oil
1–2 tbsp.	Parsley or chives, chopped
6 oz. (optional)	Bacon, sautéed crisp and diced
6 oz. (optional)	Apples, cubed
6 oz. (optional)	Smoked trout

Method

Boil or steam potatoes in their jackets.

Drain and steam dry.

Peel potatoes while still warm and slice thin.

Add oil or bacon fat.

Combine vinegar, broth, onions, salt, and sugar and bring to a boil.

Simmer 5 minutes.

Add boiling broth to bowl with potatoes and toss a few times to release the starch. (The broth should come to 1 inch below the surface of the potatoes.)

Let potatoes sit for 1 to 2 hours. Adjust seasonings and sprinkle with chives or parsley before serving.

Note: If bacon is used, sauté until crisp and drain.

If you should win the lottery, you may serve the salad with shaved white truffles.

Strawberries and Melon
with Chocolate Ice Cream
(2 portions)

Ingredients

4 oz.	Strawberries
1 tbsp.	Sugar
2	Butter, walnut size pieces
2 tbsp.	Lemon juice
1½ oz.	Orange juice concentrate
1 tbsp.	Canned green peppercorns
1 tbsp.	Kirschwasser or Pernord
2	Cantaloupe, cut into wedges
2	Chocolate wafer (for garnish)
	Chocolate ice cream

Method

Heat butter in a sauté pan. Add sugar and caramelize.
Add lemon juice and orange juice concentrate.
Bring to a boil and add strawberries.
Add green peppercorns and Kirschwasser and flame.
Remove rind from melon wedges and season with salt and pepper.
Place melon slices on a plate opposite each other.
Place chocolate ice cream in center.
Pour strawberries on or around ice cream and decorate with a chocolate wafer.
Serve immediately.

Notes

Fritz the Kettle

Little things don't mean a lot . . . they mean everything.
                    Harvey Mackay, Entrepreneur

This story is dedicated to my friend, the late Jerry Thompson, a restaurant owner and a faculty member of The Culinary Institute of America.

Hi, my name is Fritz the Kettle. I would like to tell you a little about my background. I was handmade by an excellent craftsman who worked hard and long to make me. Some of my colleagues and I are made from strong metals like stainless steel or copper.

I used to love sitting on the shelf with my friends who were all shapes and sizes, until one day when a great chef came in and bought me from the tinsmith.

He took me on a long journey to the big city of London to a large hotel. It was here that I learned the job of cooking. My chef always prepared very tasty soups and sauces and sometimes special sweets in me. He was always mindful of me and made sure that I simmered with a smile and never become angry from lack of attention and boil.

After each use, my chef cleaned me well and would make me shiny all over again. I was the happiest kettle in the world doing what I was meant to do well.

At night when I was put back on the rack with my friends, they were always sad because their chefs never took care of them the way my chef took care of me. They were always dirty and black on the outside, sad and depressed because they were put on the fire without care. Their chefs would just go and leave them to boil angrily and collect carbon and soot. They would sometimes burn and be sad.

Their soups and sauces were never full of energy and nutrients like mine, and when it came time for them to make sweets, they always gave off some bitter flavor.

When it came for them to be cleaned, they would be left with heavy scars and scratches.

My dear friends, I only wish all the chefs could be like mine and care, so that all us pots could be shiney and happy to cook with tender loving care all the time with a smile.

Fritz the Kettle . . . have a nice day.

Asparagus Soup
(10 portions)

Ingredients

16 oz.	Fresh asparagus
3 oz.	Butter
6 oz.	Leeks (white only), julienned
3 oz.	Rice flour
2½ qt	Chicken broth
1 tsp.	Salt
½ tsp.	Sugar
3	Egg yolks
2 oz.	White wine
6 oz.	Heavy cream

Method

Peel asparagus, remove woody ends, and cut into ½-inch pieces.
Save asparagus peel.
Melt butter in a large pan.
Sweat julienne of leeks for 1 minute.
Add rice flour and sweat for 1 to 2 minutes.
Add chicken broth, mix well and bring to a boil.
Add asparagus peels, salt and sugar and simmer for 15 to 30 minutes.
Place asparagus pieces, 3 tbsp. of water, 1 tsp. butter, ½ tsp. salt, and ½ tsp.
sugar in a sauté pan, cover and braise for 15 minutes.
Strain soup through a chinoise cap or cheesecloth. Bring to a boil. Meanwhile,
combine yolks, white wine, and cream. Add some hot soup to temper the egg
mixture, then fold in the rest of the soup.
Add asparagus pieces and adjust seasoning.

Pork Chops with Braised Turnips and Potato Cake
(10 portions)

Ingredients

3 lb.	Turnips
	Water, for boiling
3 oz.	Onions, diced
6 oz.	Butter
1 tsp.	Salt
1 tsp.	Sugar
10 (7 oz. each)	Pork cutlets

Potato cakes

12 oz.	Potatoes, boiled
3 oz.	Butter
6	Egg yolks
6	Egg whites
5-6 oz.	Heavy cream
⅓ oz.	Salt
3 oz.	Butter to fry 2 oz. oil
	Salt, pepper, and flour
3 oz.	Oil
6 oz.	Bacon, julienned and blanched

Method

Peel turnips, cut into wedges and cook for 5 minutes in boiling water. Drain.
Heat butter in a casserole, add turnips, diced onions, salt and 1 tsp. sugar. Toss. Add 1 cup of water and braise covered on medium fire for 20 minutes (*al dente*) and strain. Save fond.

For potato cakes

Shred or rice potatoes.
Whip butter with egg yolk and cream until creamy. Fold in shredded potatoes. In another pan, whip egg whites and salt until stiff and fold into potato mixture.
Heat butter and oil in cast iron pan.
Spoon tablespoon size dumplings into hot fat and fry until golden on each side.

Remove and keep warm.

Season pork chops with salt and pepper.

Dust with flour. Heat oil and sauté to desired doneness.

Remove from pan and add drained turnips with 2 oz. butter, ⅓ sugar, some freshly ground pepper and some more salt. Caramelize for 3 minutes.

Remove turnip, add reserved fond and reduce to maple syrup consistency. Add blanched bacon.

Arrange pork chops, turnips, and potato cake on plate, spoon sauce over it and serve.

Shrimp and Beer in a Crock
(10 portions)

Ingredients

60	Shrimp, with shells
4 oz.	Onions, sliced
7 oz.	Carrots, sliced
6 oz.	Butter
1½ pt.	Light beer
1 pt.	Chicken broth
1	Bouquet garni (parsley, thyme, bay leaves)
1	Sachet (12 crushed peppercorns, ⅓ tsp. caraway seeds, and 1 lemon peel)
To taste	Salt
1–2 oz.	White breadcrumbs, freshly ground
1–2 tbsp.	Parsley, chopped

Method

Heat butter in a pot.

Sauté carrots and onions for 2 to 3 minutes until translucent.

Add shrimp and sauté for 3 to 4 minutes.

Add beer, chicken broth, the bouquet garni, the sachet, some salt, and simmer covered for 6 minutes.

Remove shrimp and cool.

Peel shrimp and place in a large crock. Crush or chop shrimp shells and add to simmering broth. Simmer for 10 more minutes, strain and reduce by ½ or ⅔.

Add breadcrumbs to thicken and fold in some fresh butter. Adjust seasoning and pour over shrimp. Garnish with parsley.

Serve with rice or garlic bread.

Fruit Cake or Clafouti
(12 portions)

Ingredients

4 lb.	Cherries or any type of berry
7 oz.	Butter
7 oz.	Sugar
6	Egg yolks
5 oz.	Hazelnuts or walnuts, grated
9 oz.	Cake crumbs
⅓ oz.	Cinnamon
A touch	Cloves, powdered
1	Zest of lemon, grated
6	Egg whites
2 tbsp.	Kirschwasser
Some	Confectioners' sugar

Method

Preheat oven to 350 degrees F.

Line a springmold pan with 1 oz. of butter and 1 oz. of cake crumbs

Remove stems and stones from cherries or clean berries.

Whip half of the butter and half of the sugar until creamy and slowly fold in egg yolks, hazelnuts, cake crumbs, cinnamon, cloves and lemon zest.

Whip egg whites with rest of sugar until stiff and fold into cake mixture. Season with Kirschwasser and fold in cherries or berries. Place in prepared pan and bake for 50–60 minutes

Remove from oven and dust with confectioners' sugar.

Serve with whipped cream or ice cream.

Can be served hot or cold.

The Apprenticeship or Wake Up and Smell the Coffee

Bavaria 1946. I was 11 years old. The war was over and a regiment of American soldiers came into my school and set up their field kitchen. The chef's name was George. The only word he knew in German was "*Godem Scheister Bub.*" George was responsible for my desire to become a chef. He allowed me to help in the kitchen. I remember him making batter for the pancakes and showing me how to flip them. I had never seen or tasted anything like them. I can still remember the beautiful color, the light texture, and the taste. Oh, that taste still tingles on my lips!

Three years later I started my apprenticeship. My first chef was Anna Eichner, a top professional. Anna was tough on the outside, but tender on the inside. I have modeled my professional life after hers. One of my first assignments was to clean the floor and walls of the meat refrigerator every day. The refrigerator was far away from the chef's eyes, so I started a poker game in the refrigerator instead of cleaning. Well, I was caught!

The chef called me to her office, and I had to give my winnings and my days off to a homeless shelter. I was demoted to peeling potatoes and organizing the vegetable storeroom. After awhile this became boring, so I designed a new task: throwing raw eggs into a circle. I regret to inform you that this circle was hanging on a swinging door. I threw my first egg. The door swung open and the chef came through. Bulls eye! Smack in the middle of the chest. She walked over to me, stared into my eyes, grabbed my hand, and cupped my face to the raw egg on her chest. I still can feel the egg. All she said was "Strike two," and she assigned me to cleaning the stove and starting the fire every day.

This meant I had to start work at 3:00 A.M. She expected the stove to shine like a silver dollar. It was hard work, and I had to have everything ready by 7:00 A.M. when the chef arrived. She was never satisfied, and I became aggravated and began to have second thoughts about my chosen profession. George never made me clean like this! That's when I read about an acid used by plumbers to clean steel pipes. Well, I obtained a sample, but I knew it was the wrong cleaning solution to use. When I poured it on the stovetop and brushed it all over with a mop.

The stove became beautiful and shiny, but the mop dissolved. I was proud and finally successful! The stove as clean, the fire was going, and she was pleased.

I heard her mutter "Finally!" and she went to her office. Then, as the stove got hotter and hotter, small holes suddenly appeared and a terrible aroma began to develop. As the fire continued to get hotter, the holes became larger and the aroma began to stink. The chef, her nostrils wide open, stormed into the kitchen and said "*Da ist ja hopfen und maltz verloven,*" which means she lost her confidence in me. She called me the worst, most stupid, lazy, dumb apprentice she ever had. She said, "I should fail you, you know. What's your answer?"

This was fifty years ago. I realized that I must change, and I did. Fifteen years after my apprenticeship, I visited my chef, and she called me her star pupil. I asked her if she regretted my poor performance. She smiled and said "Nobody's perfect. I had to shock you into changing your attitudes. Never regret your past mistakes. Change them and help others to overcome theirs."

The moral of the story is: analyze, understand, and have passion. Respect others as you would respect yourself.

Thank you, Chef.

Chocolate Skewers

Ingredients

1	Apple, cut into wedges
1 square	Milk chocolate bar
4 slices	Rye bread with caraway seeds
4	Lean bacon, sautéed crisp
Some	Lemon juice
	Wood skewers

Method

Wash apples and cut into wedges, removing the core and seeds.
Sprinkle with lemon juice.
Break chocolate into squares.
Toast rye bread and cut into squares.
Cut bacon into squares and sauté crisp.
Skewer alternating all items.
Serve as a snack.

Boiled Moularde Duck with Horseradish Sauce and Red Beets
(4 portions)

Duck and Broth

Ingredients

2	Moularde duck breasts
2	Celery stalks, peeled and cubed
2	Carrots, peeled and cubed
1	Leek (white part only), rinsed well and sliced coarsely
2	Onions, quartered
2	Bay leaves
1 tbsp.	Black peppercorns
2	Garlic cloves
1 tbsp.	Salt

Method

Place all ingredients except duck in a large pot.
Add water and salt and simmer for 30 minutes.
Add duck breast and simmer an additional 30 minutes or until tender.
Remove duck and strain broth.

Red Beets

Ingredients

4 small	Beets
2 tbsp.	Red wine vinegar
1 tsp.	Caraway seeds
Some	Salt
2	Horseradish sticks, peeled and grated

Method

Preheat oven to 400 degrees F.
Peel beets and place each on a square of aluminum foil.
Season with vinegar, caraway seeds, salt, and horseradish.
Wrap, sealing airtight, and bake in preheated oven for 50 minutes.

Horseradish Sauce

Ingredients

1 qt.	Duck broth
Some	Salt
½ cup	Heavy cream
3 oz.	Butter
1½ oz. (4 tbsp.)	White breadcrumbs
2–3 tbsp.	Horseradish, grated
Some	Salt, sugar, and pepper

Methods

Reduce duck broth by two-thirds.

Add heavy cream, butter, horseradish, and some salt. Combine and simmer for 10 minutes.

Beat with submerged blender.

Fold in breadcrumbs to thicken.

Season with salt, pepper, and sugar.

To finish, unmold beets and cut into slices. Place sauce on plate and fan out beet slices. Sprinkle with some grated horseradish and place sliced duck on top. Garnish with dill or watercress.

Chicken in Paprika Cream Sauce
(4 portions)

Ingredients

2	Roasting chickens, cut into 8 pieces
4	Tomatoes, blanched, peeled, seeded, and cubed
4	Shallots, peeled and diced
6 oz.	Raw bacon, coarsely chopped
2	Cucumbers, peeled, seeded, and cut into 1- to 2-inch pieces
1	Roasted green pepper, peeled, seeded, and cut into ½-inch pieces
1	Roasted red pepper, peeled, seeded, and cut into ½-inch pieces
1 tsp.	Tarragon, chopped
1	Carrot, small, sliced
1	Celery stalk, sliced
1 cup, plus some	White wine
1 cup	Chicken stock
1½ cups	Sour cream
To taste	Salt and pepper
1	Twig of thyme
1–2	Garlic cloves, peeled
3 tsp.	Sweet paprika
1 tsp.	Sharp paprika
2 oz.	Tomato paste or 4 tbsp. of tomato ketchup
Some	Lemon juice
⅓ cup	Brandy

Method

Preheat oven to 450 degrees F.

Split chicken, remove backbone, and cut chicken into 8 pieces.

Heat oil, add chopped backbone, neck, and gizzards and sauté for 1 to 2 minutes, but do not brown.

Add celery, carrots, and shallots and sweat for 3 to 4 minutes.

Add paprikas, tomato paste, white wine, and chicken stock and reduce by two-thirds. Strain through a sieve.

Add sour cream and bring to a boil.

In a large sauté pan, heat some oil.

Season chicken with salt and pepper and sear chicken pieces.

Add thyme and garlic cloves and roast in preheated oven for approximately 15–20 minutes or until chicken is golden.

Add chicken and red and green peppers to sauce and simmer for 10-15 minutes.

Season with salt, pepper, and some lemon juice. Finish with brandy, some white wine, and tarragon.

Cook cucumbers in salt water until al dente. Drain, season with salt and pepper, and use to garnish plate.

Three Ways To Cook Shrimp
(4 portions)

Fried Shrimp

Ingredients

6 tbsp.	Oil
½ cup	Scallions, diced
2	Garlic cloves, coarsely chopped
1 tsp.	Fresh ginger, sliced
16 large	Raw shrimp, peeled
2 tsp.	Sugar
½ tsp.	Salt
2 tbsp.	Rice wine
2 tsp.	Vinegar
Some	Black pepper
2 tsp.	Arrowroot
3 tbsp.	V8 juice

Method

Heat oil in a wok and fry scallions, garlic, and ginger.
Add shrimp and stir-fry for about 2 minutes.
Add sugar, salt, rice wine, vinegar, and black pepper.
Dilute arrowroot with V8 juice and pour over shrimp. Cook for 2 minutes.
Serve with rice croquettes.

Shrimp in Sherry Wine
(4 portions)

Ingredients

16 large	Raw shrimp, peeled and deveined
1½ cup	Chicken broth
½ tsp.	Salt
2 tsp.	Sugar
4 oz.	Broccoli rosettes
4 tbsp.	Cooked rice
Some	Black pepper
6 tbsp.	Dry sherry
1 tbsp.	Arrowroot

Method

Place shrimp into chicken broth and simmer for 2 to 3 minutes.

Remove and keep warm.

Season broth with salt, sugar, pepper, and 5 tbsp. of sherry.

Dissolve arrowroot with 1 tbsp. of sherry and add to broth. Simmer until broth is clear.

Add broccoli rosettes and simmer for 5 additional minutes.

Add shrimp and adjust seasoning.

Serve with rice in 4 soup plates.

Chili Shrimp
(4 portions)

Ingredients

16 large	Raw shrimp
1	Egg white (save yolk for other recipes)
Some	Salt
3 tbsp.	Arrowroot
Some	Oil, for frying
3	Fresh chili peppers, seeded and chopped fine
2	Garlic cloves, sliced
1 tsp.	Sugar
1 tbsp.	Fresh ginger, shredded
¼ cup	Soy sauce
¼ cup	Sherry

Method

Peel shrimp and butterfly.
Devein and rinse.
Dry on a paper towel and place in a bowl.
Add egg whites.
Season with salt and arrowroot.
Toss until all shrimps are covered by a solid layer of salt and arrowroot.
Heat frying oil in a wok and fry shrimp for 3 to 4 minutes.
Remove.
Pour frying oil out of wok and save for another use.
Stir fry the chili peppers and sliced garlic and add all remaining ingredients.
Bring to a boil.
Add shrimp and simmer for 1 to 2 minutes.
Serve with boiled rice.

Notes

The Master Chef Examination

Opportunity never seems to be where we are. It always appears to be somewhere else. The truth is, however, that 9 out of 10 times opportunity is right in your own backyard.

We often are like the young man who sold the old family homestead: he could see no future in owning it, so he traveled the world to seek his fortune. Many years later he returned, old and poor, just to have a last look at the old home and he found that new owner had discovered gold.

My opportunity to make an impact came at the beginning of an American Certified Master Chef Test: 10 days of cooking and management examinations based on the culinary basic fundamentals and sound business techniques. I remember it well. I had prepared myself well, or in other words, I had a good mental mise en place.

When exam day came, I remembered my first class when a master chef gave the orientation. His exact words, which I have never forgotten, were "Cook with your heart, show passion, and follow the basic fundamentals set forth by our culinary masters." In all my exams, I relied on that concept. It helped me pass all my subjects. There was one time, however, that I struggled. In classical cuisine, I had picked a menu by lottery that included Consommé Diane. The directions were on page 75 of *Escoffier's Guide to Modern Cooking.* Since we were allowed to have the book with us during the test, I decided to refresh my memory and open the book. To my surprise, page 75 was not to be found! It had disappeared! I lost my cool and threw the book, and lo and behold, it ended up in the middle of the garbage can where it sank immediately! I left it there for the test, but picked it up as I left. (By the way, I passed.) The book was slippery and completely covered with garbage. I opened it and there was page 75 back where it always was. I learned a lesson that day: always take your time, don't let stress get to you, and organize your backup.

Another incident occurred during a test when I was assigned to roast a beef tenderloin and one of the main garnishes was a mushroom filled with duxelles. My standing direction to my student assistant, given in jest, was "Do not throw anything into the garbage; throw it behind the range or out the windows." (One of the master chefs was very particular about garbage.) But back to the duxelles. I chopped all the mushrooms and had them cooking. Then I saw it. I had forgotten to take the stems out of the mushroom caps. The master chef was coming towards me; there was no way to throw them out the window or behind the range! So I took them out just in time and let them disappear into my pockets.

Whew! I wiped the sweat. The master passed by. I kept cooking and I forgot about the mushroom stems. That night I threw my pants into the washing machine. My punishment came the next day when I put my hands in my pockets. That was 20 years ago, and I still remember the feeling.

I passed the test, but it showed my weaknesses and my strengths. It also made me a more understanding and passionate chef and teacher.

The moral of this story is to strive for success. Don't sell out; go for it. There is gold in being a certified master chef.

California Yellow Herbed
Potatoes and Garlic Spread
(4 portions)

Ingredients

14 large	Garlic cloves, peeled and roasted
4 tbsp.	Olive oil
1½ lb.	Potatoes, peeled
¼ cup	Scallions, chopped
3 tbsp.	Fresh basil leaves, chopped
2 tbsp.	Fresh chives, chopped
1 tbsp.	Lemon juice
1 tbsp.	Shallots, chopped
½ cup	Sour cream
To taste	Freshly ground pepper
Some	salt

Method

Preheat oven to 400 degrees F.

Place peeled garlic cloves into a sauté pan, add oil, sprinkle with salt and pepper and toss.

Roast in oven for approximately 30 minutes or until golden brown.

Cool and remove.

Peel and mash with a fork. Save oil.

Cook potatoes in jackets until tender and peel.

Mash potatoes together with garlic, add 3 tbsp. of saved oil, scallions, basil, chives, shallots and sour cream.

Add salt and pepper.

Serve as a dip with blanched vegetables or as spread.

Catfish with Chili Kraut
(4 portions)

Ingredients

1	Red pepper
1	Yellow pepper
1	Onion, finely diced
1–2	Garlic cloves
2 tbsp.	Oil
1 tbsp.	Chili powder
8 oz.	Fresh sauerkraut, rinsed
4	Oven-roasted tomatoes (or sundried)
	Salt and pepper
1 branch	Thyme
1	Bay leaf
1½ pt.	Chicken broth
3 tbsp.	Tomato ketchup
1 small	Potato, peeled
4 (6 oz.)	Fillets of catfish
	Salt and pepper
	Lemon juice
	Oil for sautéing
1	Garlic clove
1 branch	Thyme
4 tbsp.	Butter
1	Shallot, diced
1 tbsp.	Parsley, chopped

Method

Wash peppers and quarter lengthwise, remove seeds and cut into large pieces.
Crush garlic. Heat butter and sauté garlic, onions, and peppers.
Add sauerkraut, tomatoes, a sachet (thyme, bay leaf, and chili powder) and broth and cook for 60 minutes. (Add more broth if needed.)
Grate potatoes, add to sauerkraut, and bring to a boil.
Adjust seasoning and remove sachet.
Salt and pepper catfish and season with lemon.
Heat oil and sear.

Reduce heat. Add peeled garlic and thyme. Sauté for 5 to 8 minutes.
Remove fillet, garlic, and herbs.
Add butter, melt and add shallots and parsley and sauté for 2 minutes.
Presentation: Place chili kraut on plates, top with catfish and pour butter mix on top and decorate with a branch of thyme.

Pork Medallions on Eggplant, Zucchini, and Tomatoes (approximately 4 portions)

Ingredients

2 (approximately 2 lbs.)	Tenderloins of pork
1 lb.	Tomatoes
8 oz.	Zucchini
8 oz.	Japanese eggplant
1 oz.	Olive oil
2 oz.	Butter

For tomato sauce

½ cup	Tomato juice
12	Basil leaves
1 small	Onion, finely chopped
1 small	Garlic clove, mashed
2 tbsp.	Olive oil
Some	Thyme, chopped
1	Parsley stem
1	Basil stem
Some	Salt and pepper
4 tbsp.	Heavy cream
2 tbsp.	Butter

Method

For vegetables

Blanch tomatoes and peel.
Cut into quarters and deseed (save tomato water).
Cut basil leaves into strips.
Slice zucchini and eggplants thinly.
Heat olive oil and sauté zucchini and eggplants on both sides.
Remove vegetables and keep warm. Add tomatoes and warm.

For sauce

Add olive oil to pan and sauté onions and garlic for 2 minutes.
Add tomato juice and reserved tomato water (without seeds), basil, and parsley stems, some salt and pepper.
Bring to a boil and simmer for 5 minutes. Set aside.

For pork

Trim pork tenderloin and cut into twelve 2–3 oz. medallions.
Flatten lightly and season with salt and pepper.
Heat butter and sauté medallions for 3 minutes on each side. Just before finishing, add basil leaves.
Remove and keep warm.
Add tomato sauce to sauté pan.
Bring to a boil and fold in heavy cream and butter.
Adjust seasoning.
Arrange eggplant, zucchini, eggplant, zucchini, tomato quarters, eggplant in a circle.
Arrange medallions in the center and cover with tomato sauce.
Sprinkle with chopped parsley.
Serve with rice pilaf or pasta.

Warm Open Lemon Pie
with Crushed Strawberries

Ingredients

Use one greased 10-inch pie mold

Filling

17 oz.	Crème fraiche
3 whole	Eggs and 1 egg yolk
3 oz.	Sugar
Juice of 2	Lemons
Zest of 3	Lemons, grated

Dough

9 oz.	Flour
Touch of	Salt
4½ oz.	Butter
1 tsp.	Milk
3½ oz.	Sugar
2	Egg yolks

Garnish

1 pt.	Strawberries, crushed
2 tbsp.	Sugar
½ cup	Heavy cream, whipped

Method

Preheat oven to 400 degrees F.

Filling

Place crème fraiche into a bowl.
Add eggs and whip.
Add sugar, lemon juice, and grated lemon zest, mix well and rest for 2 hours in the refrigerator.

Pie dough

Combine all items and knead into a dough.
Let rest 30 minutes in refrigerator. (There will be extra dough. Freeze remainder for use later.)

Garnish

Crush strawberries and mix with sugar.
Whip heavy cream.

Assembly

Roll out dough approximately ¼-inch thick.
Set into the greased pie mold and pierce with fork.
Outline the pie with parchment paper and top with legumes to weigh dough down.
Bake in preheated oven for approximately 20 minutes.
Remove and cool.
Remove legumes and paper.
Fill baked pie shell with lemon filling and bake in a 250-degree-F oven for 60–70 minutes.
Rest for 20 minutes.
Cut into portions.
Arrange on a platter with strawberries.
Garnish with whipped cream.

Hungarian Goulash Soup
(2 portions)

Ingredients

7 oz.	Beef tenderloin, cubed into ½-inch pieces
⅓ tsp.	Caraway seeds, chopped
1 oz.	Oil
Some	Salt, pepper, and marjoram
1 oz.	Brandy
½ oz.	Bacon, diced
1 oz.	Shallots, finely chopped
1 tsp.	Hungarian paprika
2 oz.	Red pepper, cubed
2 oz.	Potatoes, cubed
⅓ tsp.	Dry marjoram
2 tbsp.	Tomato ketchup
½ tsp.	Cornstarch
½ cup	Beer
1 cup	Chicken stock
3 tbsp.	Sour cream

Method

Heat oil.

Season beef cubes with salt, pepper, caraway, and sear with bacon.

Remove from pot.

Add shallots and sauté for 1 minute.

Add tomato ketchup and brown for 2 minutes.

Add paprika and cornstarch and sauté for 30 seconds.

Add red wine, chicken stock and beer, red pepper, marjoram, and potatoes and simmer for 6 to 8 minutes.

Add seared beef and bacon.

Adjust seasoning and serve with sour cream and garlic bread.

Fillet Guljas with Spaetzle
(2 portions)

Ingredients

16 oz.	Beef tenderloin, cubed into 1-inch pieces (use tenderloin tip)
1 oz.	Oil
1–2 tsp.	Salt, marjoram, some chopped caraway seed, grated lemon zest, some coriander, some garlic, (approx. 1–2 tsp.), some black pepper
½–1 oz.	White chocolate, grated
2 tbsp.	Red bell pepper, finely cubed
6 oz.	Onions, diced very fine
1–2 tsp.	Ketchup
1 tsp.	Sweet paprika
4 tbsp.	Beer
1	Potato, peeled and cubed
3 tbsp.	Sour cream
To taste	Salt and pepper

Method

Season cubed tenderloin with salt and pepper, marjoram, caraway seeds, coriander, garlic, and lemon zest.

Heat oil, over high heat and sear cubed meat for 1 to 2 minutes.

Remove meat; keep warm.

Add onions and sauté.

Add red and yellow pepper; sauté 2 minutes.

Add paprika and chocolate and heat for 30 seconds.

Add beer and ketchup and potato and simmer until soft. (20 minutes.)

Add sour cream and beef. Do not boil.

Adjust season.

Serve with spaetzle and Boston lettuce leaves with dill vinaigrette.

Note: Pork, lamb, or turkey can be substituted.

The Critique

My second job in America was in a large hotel in New York City as a prep cook. My English was still in the infancy stage. Luckily there were many others in the same predicament, so we used a lot of sign language. The chef, Arno Schmidt, was from Austria, and his discipline and understanding helped me and many others to move up the professional ladder. It was a time of learning and listening. One of the first things I realized was that learning is easy; listening is not. Therefore, I'd like to apologize to all my chefs for not listening, as I have learned that listening is the most important skill while growing up, especially in our profession.

Well, let me get to the center of my story. It was a Tuesday that I'll never forget. The sauce cook called in sick, and I was assigned to take his place. My head swelled and my ego rose. I started to change everything because I knew better. I prepared all the sauces including a tomato sauce. I was so proud I called everybody to taste "My Tomato Sauce." As a matter of fact, I told everybody how good it was. Most of them smelled it and said "That's ok." I felt great; it was good. Then I cornered my friend Joe Tarantino whom was the pastry chef and had him taste the sauce. His face turned red, his eyes rolled, he looked for a spittoon, and then he spit *my sauce* into the garbage can and told me how terrible the sauce was. He said the sauce had no color, was pasty, and did not taste like tomato sauce. He told me to burn the recipe. I saw red. I got so upset that I lunged at him. How dare he insult my sauce and me? I though he was a friend! He just walked away. I followed him. I wanted an apology because my ego was hurt, but he just let me stand there. After all, he was a pastry chef and had dignity.

A week later he came by and asked me how I was doing, and I growled back at him. To cool me down he invited me to dinner at his home. His wife had prepared an Italian meal with meat roulades, marinara sauce, and pasta. I grudgingly went with him. It was a fantastic evening. The meal was outstanding. We had some watermelon for dessert and a couple of beers, and I realized that if I compared the pastry chef's wife's tomato sauce to mine that the chef was right. My sauce was lousy, pasty, colorless, textureless, and tasteless. I went home, ripped up my recipe, and burned it. I learned two lessons in one that night. First, only a true friend will tell you the truth, and second, always keep an open mind to new conceptions and experiences.

The moral of the story is: Always listen to criticism, don't get mad, analyze the situation, and learn. Make changes and don't let your ego interfere, and you'll become a better professional.

Tomato Soup
(4 portions)

Ingredients

2 lbs.	Tomatoes
1 qt.	Chicken broth
2 tbsp.	Butter
2 tbsp.	Flour
1 tbsp.	Salt
⅓ tbsp.	Sweet paprika
6 tbsp.	Tomato ketchup
1 tsp.	Sugar
1 or 2 bunches	Parsley
½ cup	Heavy cream, whipped
4 tbsp.	Garlic bread croutons or Swiss cheese croutons

Method

Cut tomatoes into quarters and place in a casserole and steam for 10 minutes and pass through a food mill.

Make a roux: heat butter, add flour, and stir well over a medium fire.

Add pureed tomatoes and chicken broth and ketchup.

Bring to a boil. Reduce heat and simmer for 10 minutes.

Season with salt, paprika, and sugar.

Add finely chopped parsley.

Fold in whipped cream.

Adjust seasoning.

Serve with garlic croutons or cheese croutons.

Note: To make cheese croutons: Shred Swiss cheese. Heat a Teflon pan and drop 1 oz. amounts of grated cheese into pan. Melt and brown. Turn and remove from pan. Chill.

Loin of Fallow Deer Wrapped in Savoy Cabbage

Ingredients

2	Saddle of fallow deer loin
1 head	Savoy cabbage
1	Pig caul soaked in cold water

Method

Preheat oven to 350–375 degrees F.

Season loin with salt and pepper. Sear and cool.

Blanch Savoy cabbage leaves and shock in ice water. Dry leaves.

Place soaked pig caul on a moist cheesecloth. Top with Savoy cabbage leaf and spread with duxelles (see below). Place the seared loin onto the center and top with duxelles. Roll to enclose the pig caul.

Slide on an oiled sheet pan and roast for 10 to 15 minutes.

Remove from oven and allow loin to rest for 5 minutes before slicing.

Duxelles

Ingredients

2 oz.	Butter
1 oz.	Tomato puree
4 oz.	White wine
1 oz.	*Glace de viande* (optional)
16 oz.	*Mie de pain* (white breadcrumbs)
16 oz.	Ham, cooked and minced
32 oz.	Mushrooms, minced
3 oz.	Shallots, minced
2	Egg yolks
To taste	Parsley, salt, and pepper

Method

Heat butter in a sauté pan and add shallots. Sauté until translucent.

Add ham, mushrooms, tomato puree, *glace de viande*, wine, and egg yolks. Reduce to desired thickness. Bind with *mie de pain*. Season with salt and pepper. Finish with parsley.

Serve with juniper cream sauce (page 219), potato sausages (page 220), and shallots and pears, page 221.

Juniper Cream Sauce
(3 cups)

Ingredients

3 tbsp.	Butter
1 cup	Fresh mushrooms, sliced
3 tbsp.	Shallots, finely chopped
1 qt.	Beef gravy or brown sauce
2 cups	Dry white wine
10–20	Juniper berries, crushed and tied in cheesecloth sachet
To taste	Salt and pepper
1 cup	Heavy whipping cream
3 tbsp.	Red currant jelly
2 tbsp.	Gin

Method

Melt butter in a medium saucepan.

Add mushrooms and shallots; cook over medium heat 5 minutes or until tender.

Add beef gravy, wine, and juniper berry sachet.

Simmer over medium heat until liquid is reduced by half.

Season with salt and pepper to taste.

Meanwhile, in a small mixing bowl, with mixer at medium speed, beat heavy cream until stiff peaks form.

Strain reduced sauce; return to saucepan.

Stir in red currant jelly and cook over low heat until jelly is dissolved.

Stir in gin.

Remove from heat.

Gently fold in whipped cream

Add salt and pepper to taste.

Potato Sausage

Ingredients

1 lb.	Russet potatoes, peeled, cut into quarters
2 tbsp.	Onion, finely diced
3 oz.	Smoked bacon, finely diced
3 oz.	Sauerkraut, squeezed dry and chopped
3 oz.	Clarified butter
3	Egg yolks
To taste	Salt, pepper, nutmeg, and freshly crushed coriander
	Flour or cornstarch to dust hands

Method

Cook potatoes until tender, drain and dry in oven, and put through a ricer.
Sauté the onion and bacon until translucent.
Combine the potatoes, onions, sauerkraut, egg yolks, and flour and work into a smooth dough
Season with salt, pepper, nutmeg, and coriander.
Roll into finger-size sausages. Pan fry potato sausages in clarified butter until golden brown.

Red Wine Cider with Shallots and Pears

Ingredients

6	Pears (peeled, cored, and halved)
6 large	Shallots (peeled and halved)
1 pt.	Red wine
1 tbsp.	Sugar to taste
2	Whole cloves
½ stick	Cinnamon
1	Juice of lemon

Method

Poach shallots and pears in above marinade until fork tender.

Shredded Chicken in Red Wine Sauce
(4 portions)

Ingredients

1 lb.	Chicken breast, without bone or skin and shredded
3 tbsp.	Oil
1 tbsp.	Shallots, finely chopped
2 tbsp.	Bacon, chopped
⅓ tsp.	White pepper
½ tsp.	Salt to taste
1 tsp.	Powdered chanterelles (optional)
2 tbsp.	Dried mushrooms
½ cup	Red wine
½ cup	Chicken stock
¾–1 tsp.	Arrowroot or cornstarch
2–3 tbsp.	Whipped cream
1 tbsp.	Chives, chopped
4 small	Tomatoes
½ tsp.	Onion powder
To taste	Pepper from the pepper mill

Method

Season shredded chicken with powdered chanterelles, salt, and pepper, and toss with dried mushrooms.
Heat 2 tbsp. of oil and sear chicken and mushrooms for 2 minutes.
Remove from sauté pan, keep warm.
Add bacon or shallots to pan and sauté golden.
Add arrowroot and red wine.
Reduce by two-thirds, add chicken stock and reduce to maple syrup consistency.
Add chicken and mushrooms back to pan.
Bring to a boil.
Fold in whipped cream and sprinkle with chopped chives.
Serve with mashed potatoes or pasta.

Notes

My Story about Working for the Other CIA

About 25 years ago I was assigned to teach on a Holland American cruise ship on a world tour. I had to go on board in Cartahena, Columbia. It was a very cold December day when I left Kennedy Airport on a Colombian airline. I was dressed for the occasion: long underwear, Loden mantle, and Tyrolian hat. I looked good. The temperature was below 0°F, but when I arrived in Cartahena, it was 90°F in the shade. I started to sweat heavily, and there I stood all alone on the small airport tarmac with palm trees all around me.

Suddenly I was taken to a wall and asked to spread my legs. I felt hands all over me. All that sweating must have made me look guilty. With gusto, my assailants asked me to open my suitcases. I had knives packed in between my suits, socks, and other things, and I stood with my biggest knife in my hand in an attack position. They thought I must be an assassin with my Loden mantle, Tyrolian hat, sunglasses, and sweat. I looked very suspicious, so they took me to a holding cell. After I shed all my suspicious Bavarian trimmings, I looked around. What I saw wasn't pretty. A toilet, brown from dust and dirt, a rusty wire bed, and writing on the wall. I am used to hotel toilets and soft beds. I felt like the Duke of Monte Cristo, never to be found. So I screamed, "Get me the president, the vice president, the ambassador! Get me somebody! I am an American citizen!"

After some time, I heard Spanish voices. Suddenly a figure appeared out of nowhere. A fellow with sunglasses (Army issue), baggy pants, and a tropical jacket appeared in front of me. He looked me over from top to bottom and vice versa. He said. "Yuse guys are always lousing up." I said, "What do you mean? I am a chef and chefs make no mistakes. They only make new creations. I work for The Culinary Institute of America (the good CIA)." He mumbled "OK" and left. There was a lot more talking in Spanish in raised voices. He came back and said everything was OK. "Well," I said, "am I going to my hotel?" He said "No, but we will send you a mattress, sheets, soft toilet paper, and dinner. Tomorrow they will take you to the ship."

The next morning I was taken to the ship by jeep with a motorcycle escort in front and back. It looked very impressive. At the ship everyone thought I was a VIP. I quickly went on board and gave them the international sign of the extended finger. I am a very nosy person, so I investigated the situation and found that the person that arranged my trip wrote down "works for the CIA" rather than spelling out"The Culinary Institute."I am very happy it turned out well, and I was allowed to go on with my lectures on the ship and see the Panama Canal, but the thing I really remember is the brown spot on . . . you know what I mean.

Believe it or not.

Clear Tomato Soup Peru

Ingredients

8	Ripe tomatoes, coarsely cubed
1 cup	Cucumber, peeled and diced
1	Garlic clove, peeled
8	Basil leaves
To taste	Salt, pepper, and lime juice

Method

Put tomatoes, garlic, basil leaves, and cucumber through a juicer.

Place in a sauce pan and bring to a boil.

Season with lime juice, salt, and pepper, and strain through a linen cloth and cool.

To garnish, use one of the following: peeled, seeded, and diced tomatoes sautéed with shallots and garlic; diced, peeled and seeded cucumber; minced red onion; diced yellow and red peppers blanched for 2 to 3 minutes in tea; chiffonade of basil; and a drizzle of extra virgin olive oil.

Place clear tomato broth in a soup cup or plate.

Finish with chosen garnish.

Serve with finger sandwiches (see page 228).

Shrimp Finger Sandwich

Ingredients

12 oz.	Cooked shrimp, diced
2 tbsp.	Mayonnaise
2 tbsp.	Sour cream
1 tbsp.	Dill, chopped
6 slices	Rye toast, thinly sliced
2–3 oz.	Alfalfa sprouts

Method

Combine shrimp with mayonnaise, sour cream, and dill. Season with salt and pepper.
Place on side of toast bread down.
Place on thin layer of shrimps down.
Top with other slice of toast.
Cut into small, rectangular finger sandwiches.
Top sandwiches with alfalfa sprouts or other desired garnish.

Mushroom Ragout with Rice Pilaf
(4 portions)

Ingredients

2 lb.	Mushrooms (any type)
2	Onions, diced fine
3 oz.	Butter
To taste	Salt and pepper
2	Egg yolks
1 cup	Heavy cream
½ cup	White wine
3 tbsp.	Parsley, chopped

Method

Rinse mushrooms and slice.
Dice onion fine.
Heat butter and sweat onions until translucent (2 to 3 minutes).
Add mushrooms, white wine and cook over medium heat for 20 minutes.
Season with salt and pepper.
Combine cream and egg yolk. Mix well and fold into mushrooms.
Bring to a boil.
Add chopped parsley.
Adjust seasoning.
Serve with rice pilaf.

Spare Ribs with Pepper Salad
(4 portions)

Ingredients

1	Red pepper, julienned
1	Yellow pepper, julienned
1	Green pepper, julienned
1 large	Red onion, sliced thin
1 pt.	Water
1 tsp.	Salt
1 branch	Thyme
10 tbsp.	Vinegar
5 tbsp.	Olive oil
2 lb.	Spare ribs
3 tbsp.	Soy sauce
2 tbsp.	Honey
3 tbsp.	Worcestershire sauce
A touch	Cayenne pepper
½ tsp.	salt

Method

Combine water with salt, thyme, and vinegar and bring to a boil.
Add peppers and onion.
Bring to a boil and remove from heat. Chill vegetables in cooking liquid.
Drain vegetables and toss with oil (adjust seasonings and acidity).
Combine soy sauce, honey, Worcestershire sauce, cayenne, salt, some oil, and brush on spare ribs.
Place ribs in a covered container and let them rest in refrigerator overnight.
Place ribs on grill or bake in oven approximately 50 minutes.
Serve with pepper salad and Italian bread.

Steamed Dumplings Bavarian Style

Ingredients

16 oz.	Flour
¾ oz. (or 1 packet)	Yeast
4 oz. (½ cup)	Lukewarm milk
3 oz. (2 tbsp.)	Sugar
3 oz.	Butter
2	Eggs
Touch	Salt

To cook

4 oz.	Butter
6 tbsp.	Sugar
8 oz.	Milk

Method

Place flour into a bowl.

Mix well and add yeast together with half a cup of lukewarm milk and 2 tbsp. of sugar.

Rest for 20 minutes covered, then mix with rest of lukewarm milk and rest of sugar.

Add melted butter, eggs, and salt and mix into a small dough.

Beat for 3–4 minutes or until blisters develop.

Form into dumplings.

Place on a floured cheesecloth, cover with cheesecloth, and rest for 20 minutes.

Place 4 oz. butter and sugar into a flat casserole, combine lightly.

Add milk and place dumplings next to each other into the milk.

Place a moist cheesecloth on casserole and cover with a lid and finish dumplings over medium heat for 30 minutes.

Do not remove lid during the cooking process.

Remove and serve with vanilla sauce.

Note: For vanilla sauce, melt 1 pint of vanilla ice cream.

Bring to a boil.

Mix 2 eggyolks and ½ cup of heavy cream and fold under hot melted ice cream.

Bring to a boil and serve with dumplings.

The Convention or When it Rains it Pours

As in other professions, chefs have a yearly gathering called a convention. I belong to a professional organization called the American Culinary Federation, and we had a meeting of over 2,000 chefs in Houston one year. We arrived on a Thursday, and I checked into our hotel. The manager was an old friend of mine and had arranged for me to stay in the Presidential Suite, which was on the twelfth floor with a view of Houston. Just as I stepped into the lobby, all the lights went out and caused a blackout. I refused to walk up to the twelfth floor. Luckily, a friend offered his first-floor room to me temporarily.

That evening we had the black-tie Academy dinner. I changed into my tuxedo and walked out the terrace door not knowing the swimming pool was right there! Lo and behold, I fell into the pool! There was a tidal wave and the water splashed all over the terrace. I returned to the room dripping wet, and I changed by candlelight. The lights had not come on yet in the banquet hall either, and it was dark except for candlelight. There was a green candle behind me as I sat down. Suddenly the lights came back on, and there I was among the formal black tie guests with my blue jeans, green jacket, and green candle wax dripping down on my hair. It looked like I had a Mohican haircut! I was the "center cut" that evening and that was just the first day of the convention!

The next day we went to a restaurant for dinner. It was a reproduction of a 18th-century inn. We sat at long tables and the waitresses were called wenches. As I sat down, guess what happened? The chair collapsed, and I wound up sitting on the floor. They finally brought me a second chair, and I began to eat. Then, an announcement was made that for $1.00 you could go up on stage and kiss one of the girls. I looked at her; her lips were so tempting. Everyone dashed to the stage, including me. Unfortunately, as I tiptoed over the empty chairs, someone moved the last chair just as I was stepping over it. I went down like a kamikaze and the floor and walls rattled. I heard someone yell "Earthquake in Texas!" I tried to push myself up (all 340 pounds of fat muscle). I grabbed something to help me recover. It happened to be the piano player's chair and down he went with a piano bang. Finally, we both got up. Again, I was the "center cut." I never got to kiss any of the girls' lips. That was day two.

On the third day we went to a rodeo. Horses were bucking, and bulls were jumping. Halfway though the rodeo I was volunteered to be on the New York team to wrestle a cow. They gave us a pair of panties and a bra, and we were instructed to put them on the cow; the team to finish first was declared the champion. Our cow seemed to be very nervous, mooing constantly. I decided to take the bra, as I didn't want to get near the rear of the cow. I took the humongous bra and leapt off the ground like Superman, only slower. I flew towards the cow with bra in hand. The cow saw me coming and turned, and while I flew towards her, something flew out of her. I was covered in brown and started to smell like a cow. I believe there is even a video showing the encounter floating around. This was day three.

I returned to the hotel to change for dinner. This was only the second time I had an elevator all to myself. (The first time was in 1965 during the Big Blackout, but that's another story.) When I stepped in, everyone else stepped out. I threw the condemned shirt into my suitcase, simonized myself, and went to dinner. The main course was a braised Euter Ala Bonne Femme (I hope I didn't squash the cow). As the saying goes, "all good things come in threes." The next day was great, and we got to enjoy the twelfth-floor Presidential Suite. I even sat on a chair that had been sat on by either former President Nixon or former President Eisenhower. I think I felt a vibration.

The next day we flew home, and lo and behold, the airline lost my luggage. Luckily, I had the shirt with the cow's blessing in my suitcase; this helped locate my luggage immediately. I recall the delivery person wearing nose clips. Even with all these encounters, the food, hospitality, and camaraderie of the convention were perfect, and this gathering of culinarians severed its purpose of fostering friendship and sharing knowledge.

Always remember: Cooking is an art, a science, the basic fundamentals, common sense, and passion. I hope you enjoyed the story and have fun cooking with my recipes.

Hungarian Pork Stew
(4 portions)

Ingredients

1½ lb.	Pork butt, cubed
8 oz.	Onions, diced
2	Garlic cloves, mashed or minced
2 oz.	Oil
1 tbsp.	Hungarian sweet paprika
2 tbsp.	Tomato ketchup
½ cup	Earl Grey Tea
1 tsp.	Salt
3	Green peppers, seeds removed and cubed
2	Tomatoes
To taste	Finely ground black pepper

Method

Heat oil and sear pork cubes.

Add onion, garlic, paprika, tomato ketchup and tea and simmer covered for 10 minutes.

Add cubed green peppers and simmer covered for 15 to 20 minutes or until meat is tender.

Adjust seasoning.

Serve with noodles, spaetzle, or parsley potatoes, and cucumber salad.

Note: For change of taste exchange green peppers with 2 cups of rinsed sauerkraut.

No Beef Please: Potato-Crusted Salmon with Creamed Leeks and Red Wine Butter Sauce

Potato-Crusted Salmon

Ingredients

4	Salmon steaks, 2 to 3 oz. each
¾ cup	Potatoes, grated and squeezed dry
2 tbsp.	Fresh dill, chopped
3 tbsp.	Olive oil
To taste	Salt, pepper, and tea leaves

Method

Place salmon steaks on a tray and season both sides with salt, pepper, and tea leaves.

Grate potato and soak in cold water. Squeeze out excess water. Season with salt, pepper, and dill, and evenly distribute potatoes on top of the salmon steaks.

In a hot skillet, add oil and heat until smoking. Carefully place fish, potato side down, into the pan and sauté until the potatoes are crisp.

Flip salmon over and cook to desired doneness. Remove from pan and keep warm.

Creamed Leeks

Ingredients

2 cups	Leeks, diced
1 tbsp.	Whole butter
1 tbsp.	White truffle oil
½ cup	Cream
To taste	Salt and pepper

Method

Heat a skillet and add butter. Melt butter and add leeks.

Sweat leeks for 2 minutes then add cream and reduce until leeks are soft. Season with truffle oil, salt, and pepper.

Red Wine Butter Sauce

Ingredients

6 oz.	Red wine
2 oz.	Brewed Earl Gray tea
1 tbsp.	Shallots, chopped
½	Garlic clove, mashed
2 tbsp.	Cream
½ cup	Butter, cut into cubes
To taste	Salt, pepper, and sugar
	Micro greens tossed in lime juice, salt, sugar, and olive oil for garnish

Method

Heat skillet. Sweat garlic and shallots until soft.

Add red wine and tea. Reduce to about 3 tbsp. and carefully add cream.

Reduce until the liquid has the consistency of maple syrup.

Slowly incorporate whole butter cubes.

Season with salt, pepper, and sugar.

To serve: Place creamed leeks on a plate. Top with salmon and drizzle red wine sauce around the salmon. Top with marinated micro greens.

Note: For dietary reasons use arrowroot or cornstarch instead of butter to thicken.

My Mother-in-Law's Pierogies
(This should give me points with her . . .)
(yields 20)

Ingredients
Dough

11 oz.	Flour
Touch of	Salt
3 oz.	Butter
2½ oz.	Lard
2½ oz.	Sour cream
3 oz.	Water

Stuffing

14 oz.	Onions, finely chopped
3 oz.	Butter
1 lb.	Ground beef or ground sturgeon or monk fish
2	Hard-boiled eggs, chopped
2 oz.	Dill, chopped
Some	Salt and black pepper
1	Egg
Some	Milk

Method
Dough

Place flour on a cutting board, add salt, butter, and lard and work together like a pie dough.
Make a ring, add cold water to center and work quickly into a dough.
Cover with plastic wrap and rest in refrigerator for 1 hour.

Stuffing

Preheat oven to 350 degrees F.
Heat butter and sauté onion for 1 minute.
Add ground meat or fish and sauté over high heat for 5 minutes.
Place into a bowl.
Add chopped eggs and dill and season with salt and pepper.
Roll dough thinly and cut into 3-inch circles.
Combine milk and eggs and mix well (egg wash).

Brush rim of circles with egg wash, place 1 tsp. of meat or fish mix into center of the circle and fold dough over into half-moon shapes. Press dough together with the tines of a fork.

Place pierogies on a buttered sheetpan, brush with egg wash and bake in pre-heated oven for approximately 30 minutes or boil or sauté.

Notes: Stuffing can be made from fish, chicken, game, or vegetables.

Serve with Russian dressing or as a party dish.

Fresh Strawberries
with Mock Devonshire Cream
(4 portions)

Ingredients

2 pt.	Fresh strawberries
1–2 tbsp.	Sugar
3 drops	Vanilla extract
⅓ cup	Kirshwasser
1 can	Condensed milk
4	Lemon cookies
4	Mint leaves

Method

Clean strawberries. Remove stem and leaves. Cut into quarters.
Mix strawberries with sugar, vanilla and Kirschwasser.
Marinate in refrigerator for 1 to 2 hours.
Bring a pot of water to a boil and submerge the can of condensed milk.
Simmer for approximately 30 minutes.
Remove can and chill.
Arrange strawberries in a bowl and decorate with mint leaves.
Serve clotted milk and cookies on the side.

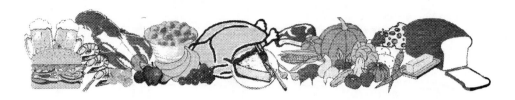

Notes

Food, the Essence of Life or the Love Story of a Century

Lobster, Homard, Hummer, Langosta. We use it for appetizers, luncheons, and dinners. We enjoy its texture, taste, and aroma but what do we really know about this interesting crustacean?

Did you know that this tasty morsel was considered a sensuous delicacy to the ancient Romans and possibly even by older civilizations? Marcus Caelius Aspicius, the famous Roman gourmet, food writer, and cook, dedicated parts of his ninth book, *The Thalassa*, to the langosta and called the lobster "stimulating." As a matter of fact, an old Roman folk tale says, "No orgy without lobster." Now, now, the tale was referring to a food orgy, of course!

Medieval Europe's legends attest that Europeans strongly believed that lobster was the "food of lovers." As marvelously shown in the film '*Tom Jones*,' they dined sensuously on lobster while sitting opposite each other in their romantic inns and taverns.

To further illustrate the strong belief in the power of food, let me tell you the story of a famous classic dish, "Filet of Sole Walewska." As history tells us, the beautiful Polish Baroness Walewska and Napoleon Bonaparte, Emperor of France, fell in love and lived together. When he lost the great war against Russia, however, he had to leave her behind. In order to communicate her feelings to Napoleon (without the aid of telephones or faxes), the Baroness ordered her chefs to create a dish using Dover sole, lobster, velouté sauce, and truffles. The recipe was sent to the Emperor.

The ingredients the baroness chose were significant because of the meaning attached to these food. Dover sole was believed to be the food of travelers; lobster was considered the food of lovers; velouté was related to satin or velvet sheets, which were considered to be the tent of the temple of marriage; and truffles had the reputation of being an aphrodisiac.

The dish was served to His Majesty in his Palace Les Invalides in Paris (named in honor of war casualties). Without words, the baroness had relayed her feelings to the emperor. She spoke to him through the food served to him. If she had used words she might have said, "You traveled many miles back to France. I love you. I feel married to you. I will always remember our good time together."

Ooh, isn't this delicious stuff, and doesn't it help us understand why food was, is, and always will be powerful? It not only feeds the body; it also feeds the mind. It is important that we as chefs understand and follow the passion our professional forefathers have left us. Every little bit, may it be a spice or herb, vegetable, meat, or fish, is important and we need to understand and remember that.

Cooking is an art, a science; it requires soul and a passion for life.

Happy Cooking!

Pickled Cucumber Soup with Chicken Klein and Rice (Rassounik is Potracha's Risoan)
(2 quarts)

Ingredients

16 oz.	Chicken klein (gizzards, necks, and wings)
1½–2 qt.	Chicken broth
3 oz.	Dill pickle marinade
2 oz.	Celery, julienned
2 oz.	Parsnips, julienned
3 oz.	Leeks (white only), julienned
2 oz.	Butter
To taste	Salt
8 oz.	Potatoes, cubed small
8 oz.	Dill pickles, sliced
3 oz.	Boiled rice
1	Egg yolk
5 oz.	Heavy cream
2 tbsp.	Dill, chopped
2 tbsp.	Parsley, chopped

Method

Combine klein, chicken broth, and pickle marinade and simmer for 1 hour, or until gizzards are tender.

Heat butter in a large pot, add onions and sauté.

Add julienned vegetables and braise for 10 minutes.

Add strained chicken broth and potatoes and simmer until tender (20 to 30 minutes).

Coarsely cut gizzards, neck and wing meat. Add with boiled rice to broth. Bring to a boil.

Add sliced dill pickles.

Combine heavy cream with egg yolk.

Remove soup from heat and fold in egg mixture. Bring to a boil.

Add dill and parsley.

This soup can be served with black pumpernickel raisin bread and dill pickles.

Fillet of Sole Walewska
(4 portions)

Ingredients

12	Fillets of Dover sole
2 tbsp. (⅓ stick)	Butter
2 tbsp.	Shallots, finely chopped
7 oz.	White wine
7 oz.	Fish broth (or chicken broth)
To taste	Salt
1	Bouquet garni (parsley stem, thyme, ½ bay leaf)
2 tbsp.	Butter
2–3 tbsp.	Flour
2	Egg yolks
¼ cup	Heavy cream
1 tbsp.	Whipped cream
8	Lobster medallions
8 slices	Truffles

Method

Preheat oven to 400 degrees F.
Season fillets with salt and pepper.
Brush a flat dish with butter. Sprinkle with finely chopped shallots.
Top with fish fillets add white wine, fish broth, and bouquet garni.
Bring to a boil.
Cover with aluminum foil or parchment paper.
Place into preheated oven for 5 to 8 minutes.
Remove fish carefully and keep warm.
Mix flour, soft butter together (beurre manir)
Reduce fish fond by half.
Add butter mixture and thicken.
Mix egg yolk and heavy cream together, fold into sauce and bring to a boil.
Finish with 1 tbsp. of whipped cream and adjust seasoning.
Place fish on oval plate.
Top with lobster medallions and cover with sauce. Decorate with a slice of truffle.
Serve with pierogies (page 238), rice, or boiled potatoes.
Note: If Dover sole is unavailable, use 4–6 oz. fillets of lemon sole.

Kawkeski Salad
(10 portions)

Salad

Ingredients

5 small	Eggplants, sliced
5 large	Tomatoes, sliced
10 oz.	Pumpkins, sliced
1 tsp.	Salt
1 tsp.	Paprika
2	Garlic cloves, finely chopped
Up to 3 oz.	Olive oil
2 oz.	Parmesan cheese
1 oz.	Breadcrumbs
Juice of ½	Lemon

Dressing

Ingredients

5	Hardboiled eggs, chopped
2 tsp.	Sharp mustard
6 tsp.	Vinegar
4–5 oz.	Sour cream
½ tsp.	Sugar or to taste
To taste	Salt and pepper
1–2 tbsp.	Dill, chopped

Method

Combine all dressing ingredients.
Preheat oven to 350 degrees F.
Slice eggplants, tomatoes, and pumpkin.
Place into a fireproof casserole and season with salt, paprika, and garlic.
Add olive oil and sprinkle with parmesan and breadcrumb mix.
Cover with aluminum foil and bake for 30 to 45 minutes.
Remove, chill, then toss with lemon juice and dressing. Serve on lettuce leaves.

Kissel (Berry Purée)
(10 portions)

Ingredients

3½ lb.	Fresh berries (raspberry, red currents, strawberries, blueberries or rhubarb)
1 pt.	Tea
5–7 oz.	Sugar
2–2½ oz.	Arrowroot
3 oz.	White wine

Method

Combine berries, Tea, and sugar.
Bring to a boil and simmer for 30 minutes.
Puree in food processor or put through food mill.
Place back on fire and bring to a boil.
Thicken with arrowroot diluted with white wine.
Fill into individual glasses and chill.
Serve with sour cream, whipped heavy cream, and garnish with sweet prune pierogie dusted with confectionary sugar (see page 58).

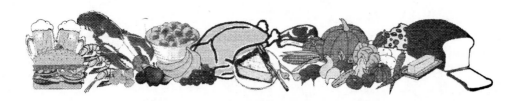

Notes

The First of April or the American Truffle

April 1st has always designated as a day to fools. Not dumb fools or intelligent fools, but just plain simple fools, and we are all in that category.

Many years ago on one first of April, my friend Tony Seta and I had an idea to fool a connoisseur, great chef, and entrepreneur known to many worldwide. He was visiting and brought a colleague with him. His or her name shall remain anonymous, but he or she will recognize him or herself from my story. I remember the chef and his colleague did not believe in American Haut Cuisine.

In the early days of my learning this glorious profession I worked with the garde manger of the Bayrischer in Munich. His name was Karl Stetzel. He was a very energetic man and a great teacher who loved his job, the ladies, and himself. I remember he never had a spot on his uniform. He was "Mr. Sanitizer." Truffles were expensive at this time, as they are today, and every buffet platter had to be decorated with them, as it is the most expensive fungus on earth. Chef Stetzel invented the "mock truffle," made from used coffee grounds, kitchen bouquet and gelatin. After mixing the ingredients well, they were formed in a shape of a truffle and refrigerated. When used as a decoration, they looked so real that we had to guard them closely because people started to eat them.

On this particular April first, Tony and I buried some of these fake morsels into the ground by the old oak trees (they unfortunately were lost when the CE building was erected). We walked out the front door of Roth Hall loaded down with a fork, shovel basket, and Tony's schnauzer pulling on the line. We couldn't get a pig. When the chefs spotted us and asked where we were going, we replied "truffle hunting." They said "Really? Truffles in America!" "Sure," we said. "Right here on our campus."

Well, we all walked over to the trees. The dog was sniffing and Tony said, "Do you see the blue flies?" (These are indigenous in France and pinpoint possible truffles in the ground.) We really poured it on. Finally, we decided to start digging, and carefully pushed the fork into the ground. The dog was panting, the birds were singing, the tension was building, and there they were—beautiful blackish brown truffles.

It was a ceremony as holy to the Jesuits performing in our Church, now called Alumni Hall; there was a halo floating above and I even saw a dove! We played it to the hilt. We marched with the chefs in tow, basket in hand, fork and shovel over our shoulders, and dog wagging his tail into the kitchen. The chefs foaming with excitement, grabbed a truffle and started to sniff it with their nostrils vibrating. Suddenly, one chef said, "I never detected coffee aroma in truffles. This must be a different type." With a serious face, Tony said, "American truffles, don't you know." Just before the chef popped one into his mouth, Tony, the dog and I shouted "April Fool!" Then there was silence. This was 20 years ago; the chef has never talked to us since.

The moral of the story is: loosen up and celebrate funny pranks as long as they are in good taste. Truffle taste, that is. Forget your ego. Laugh and have fun. Life is short, so always remember that cooking is an art, a science, and sharing.

Chopped Liver

Ingredients

5 lb.	Chicken or beef liver
2½ lb.	Onions, sliced
Some	Garlic (optional)
1–2 lb.	Chicken fat, margarine, or butter
Some	Thyme
Some	Marjoram
15	Hardboiled eggs
To taste	Salt and pepper

Method

Preheat oven to 400 degrees F.
Heat fat and sear liver and onions.
Season with garlic, salt, pepper, thyme, and marjoram.
Bake in preheated oven until cooked through.
Chill and grind through a food processor the fine blade of a meat grinder with the eggs.
Adjust seasoning.
Place mixture in a crock or a mold.
Refrigerate and decorate with truffles.
Serve with crackers.
Note: Black olives can be substituted for truffles.

Cave Pasta with Sweetbreads and Truffles
(10 portions)

Ingredients

1–2 oz.	Butter
2–3 oz.	Breadcrumbs, toasted
4 slices	Ham
1 lb.	Sweetbreads, precooked, sliced, and sautéed
5 oz.	Prunes, pitted
5 oz.	Parmesan cheese, grated
½ tsp.	Cinnamon
¼ tsp.	Nutmeg
To taste	Salt
To taste	Freshly ground pepper
2 oz.	Butter
1–2 lb.	Lasagna noodles, cooked
	Béchamel Sauce (see recipe below)

Method

Preheat oven to 400 degrees F.

Grease an oblong casserole with butter, dust with breadcrumbs, and line with pasta.

Place ham on bottom of pan.

Top ham with the sweetbreads, prunes, and half the béchamel sauce. Season with the cinnamon, nutmeg, salt, pepper, and half of the cheeses.

Top with a layer of pasta and the rest of the béchamel sauce.

Sprinkle with the remaining cheese and 2 oz. of butter and bake in a pre-heated oven for 30 minutes or until golden brown.

Let dish cool for 20 minutes and serve.

Béchamel Sauce

Ingredients

2 oz.	Butter
1½ oz.	Flour
20 oz.	Half chicken stock, half milk
To taste	Pepper, nutmeg, and salt

Method

Heat butter, add flour, and cook over medium heat for 1-2 minutes,
Add cold milk and chicken stock and stir well (no lumps). Bring to a boil
(stir once a while). Season with salt, pepper, and nutmeg, simmer for 20–30
minutes.

Note: Prunes are the poor man's truffle and can be substituted with real black
truffles.

Cold Marinated Trout Sweet and Sour
(4 portions)

Ingredients

4	Rainbow trout fillets, skinned and bones removed
Some	Salt and fresh ground pepper
2 tsp.	Sugar
1 tbsp.	Pine nuts, coarsely chopped
1–2 small	Red onion, thinly sliced
1–4 tbsp.	Raisins or currents
1 tbsp.	Capers
2 small	Carrots, scored with chanel knife and slice thinly
4 oz. (½ cup)	Vinegar
4 tbsp.	Olive oil
3 oz.	Tea
1 package	Mesclun greens
Some	Fresh dill sprigs

Method

Place trout fillets in a porcelain dish.

Season both sides with salt, pepper, and sugar.

Sprinkle pine nuts, red onions, raisins, and capers over fillets. (Reserve some to sprinkle over salad greens.)

Blanch carrots in boiling salt water then shock in ice water. Sprinkle over fish.

Pour vinegar, tea, and oil over fish and cover with plastic wrap. Marinate overnight or 12 hours in the refrigerator.

Remove trout, reserving marinade. Arrange on a platter or individual plates.

Toss greens with some of the marinade and place on platter or individual plates.

Sprinkle some of the onions, pine nuts, and capers over salad greens.

Decorate with a sprig of dill and mock truffles (black jumbo olives).

Serve with toasted pumpernickel bread.

Pork Pilaf (My Way)
(4 portions)

Ingredients

1 lb.	Pork butt, cubed
3 medium	Onions, chopped fine
4	Garlic cloves, minced
4 tbsp.	Olive oil
1 tsp.	Salt
1½ cups	Long grain rice
2½–3 cups	Chicken stock
½–1 tsp.	Ground black pepper
1 tsp.	Madras curry
1 knifetip	Ground cinnamon and powdered cloves

Method

Preheat oven to 400 degrees F.

Heat olive oil in a casserole.

Add onions and sauté for 1 minute.

Add garlic and sauté for 1 minute.

Add pork butt and sweat for 2 minutes.

Add rice and stir until coated with oil.

Add pepper, salt, curry, cinnamon, cloves.

Add chicken stock and bring to a boil.

Cover and cook in preheated oven for 20 minutes.

Check if all moisture is absorbed and rice is tender.

Stir well to loosen and remove steam.

Serve with truffle red wine sauce (see page 113), or tomato sauce (see page 208), or string bean salad. (If truffles aren't available, use plain old mushrooms.)

Index

Notes

Notes